London's Railways
From the Air

London's Railways
From the Air
Aerofilms

Ian Allan
PUBLISHING

Left: Muswell Hill, (see page 170), June 1949 (R11001)   *Above:* Cannon Street, (see page 46), 30 August 1929 (P28617)

Contents

First published 2006

ISBN (10) 0 7110 3144 4
ISBN (13) 978 0 7110 3144 9

Published by Ian Allan Publishing

an imprint of Ian Allan Publishing Ltd, Hersham, Surrey KT12 4RG;

and printed by Ian Allan Printing Ltd, Hersham, Surrey KT12 4RG.

Code: 0606/A1

Visit the Ian Allan Publishing website at www.ianallanpublishing.com

Introduction

Whilst it is possible to gain a limited perspective of the scale of the country's railway network from ground level, it is only from the air that a true appreciation of how far the railways can dominate a locality can be appreciated. The unique archive of historical aerial photographs possessed by the Aerofilms company, reproduced in this book, shows how the sheer scale of the railway industry, particularly apparent in the era before rationalisation took effect, has dominated significant parts of London. Whilst the main line railways may never have penetrated right into the heart of the city, other than via the network of underground lines, beyond the central core, and in particular around the great main line termini, the railways provided a ring of steel that was essential for the safe and efficient movement of people and freight — traffic without which London would not have been able to operate.

During its near 90-year history Aerofilms has taken countless photographs of the Greater London area, many of which feature railway stations, junctions, goods yards and locomotive sheds. Drawing upon this archive, with the earliest images dating to before the Grouping of the railways in 1923, the book includes more than 125 images portraying the many facets of railway operation in the Metropolis.

Production of the book has only been possible as a result of the co-operation of the staff at Simmons Aerofilms' office at Potters Bar, in particular the librarian Chris Mawson. To him and to the rest of the staff we'd like to express our thanks for their help.

London Bridge (see page 154). 29 September 1969 (SV2403)

Addiscombe

The line to Addiscombe, latterly a one-mile long branch from Woodside, opened from New Beckenham, on the Lewisham-New Beckenham route, on 1 April 1864, having been authorised as an extension of the Mid-Kent Railway in 1862. The Mid-Kent became part of the South Eastern Railway in 1864. The line from Woodside south to Selsdon opened in 1885. The station, known as Croydon (Addiscombe Road) until 1925, saw electric services introduced on 28 February 1926. As is evident in this photograph, the station was provided with a single two-faced platform, signalbox, four-road EMU shed (which opened with the electrification of the line in 1926) and a single-storey station building on the A222 (Addiscombe Road). Passenger services over the Woodside-Sanderstead section were withdrawn on 16 May 1983, at which time the line south from Woodside closed completely. The Addiscombe branch, however, remained open until 31 May 1997 when the branch was closed in connection with the development of the Croydon Tramlink although the EMU shed had closed five years earlier. A new station, called Addiscombe, was opened in 2000 on the Croydon Tramlink route over the former line south from Woodside. Although there were efforts to see the Addiscombe site used as a preservation base, these came to nothing.

14 August 1970 (A206734)

Addison Road (Kensington)

Dating to 1921, this view of Addison Road station is taken looking towards the west with the Grand Hall of the Olympia exhibition centre in the centre. The origins of the Grand Hall date back to 1884 when the National Agricultural Co was established to construct a hall capable of accommodating shows in London. Designed by Henry E. Coe, construction work started in July 1885 and the building was opened on 27 December 1886. A small extension to the hall — the Pillar Hall — was added in 1896 but it was not until after the date of this photograph that the site was to be expanded significantly. The National Hall was added in 1923 and the Empire Hall (later called Olympia 2) followed in 1929. In the foreground is Addison Road station — later known as Kensington Olympia — which as illustrated here was the result of rebuilding in the LNWR style in 1869. The West London Railway opened from Willesden Junction to the basin of the Kensington Canal, slightly to the south of the scene located here, on 27 May 1844. The original station serving Kensington was located slightly to the south; it was relocated to the site illustrated here in 1862. During the interwar years, passenger services to Addison Road comprised a steam shuttle provided by the SR from Clapham Junction, an LMS service from Willesden to Clapham Junction and LPTB service from Edgware Road to Addison Road which operated via Westbourne Park and a spur from the Metropolitan line that ran from Latimer Road station to the West London line. However, during the period, passenger traffic declined with the result that LMS services ceased on 3 October 1940 with those operated by the SR and LPTB being withdrawn on the 20th of the same month.

7 June 1921 (6523 [C13376])

Addison Road

A second view of Addison Road, this time taken looking towards the north, shows the dramatic development of the Olympia site over the previous 25 years. Following the station's closure in 1940, it was renamed Kensington Olympia on 19 December 1946 when a new shuttle service was introduced over the District Line from Earls Court on dates when exhibitions were held at Olympia. Running from the bay platform at the south end of the station, these services were made daily in 1986.
Also running to the station was the untimetabled 'Kenny Belle' service to Clapham Junction at peak hours; in 1968 there were two daily departures and in 1986 there were six. The importance of the route, however, has increased; between 1966 and 1982 the north end of the station was used as a Motorail terminus and from 1979 onwards the route was used by inter-regional cross-country services. Moreover, increased local services linking Clapham Junction with Willesden Junction were provided; these are now in the hands of Silverlink.
The route is also used by services operated by Southern from Brighton to Watford Junction. The station itself, however, is radically altered and the last part of the station illustrated here to survive, the ex-LNWR signalbox at the southern end of the station adjacent to the LT bay platform was demolished in the 1990s.

14 April 1949 (A22038/49)

12

Alexandra Palace

With its hilltop position, Alexandra Palace provides an excellent vantage point for views across towards Central London. Designed by J. Johnson, the Palace was opened on 24 May 1873. It has had a somewhat chequered career, having suffered severe fire damage on several occasions, and found a variety of uses (including being the location of the BBC's pioneering television broadcasts). Today it is again used in part as an exhibition centre. This view, taken looking towards the east in 1946, shows well the building and the adjacent branch railway terminus. The railway was not the only means of tracked transport to provide access; an electric tramway also served the site, although this had been withdrawn during the 1930s. The railway was promoted by the Muswell Hill Railway, which was authorised on 13 May 1864 and opened on 24 May 1873 contemporaneously with the Palace itself. The railway, however, was destined to have a relatively short life as services were suspended on 9 June, after the Palace was severely damaged by fire, and not resumed until the Palace reopened on 1 May 1875. Thereafter the Muswell Hill Railway led a somewhat precarious existence until it was taken over by the GNR in 1911. As part of the ex-GNR 'Northern Heights' section, the Alexandra Palace route was included within the proposals to electrify the route and integrate the services into the Northern Line. Although part of the work was undertaken, steam services continued to run from Finsbury Park to Alexandra Palace and, after World War 2, the proposals were dropped. Passenger services continued to serve Alexandra Palace until 5 June 1954 at which date the line between Muswell Hill and Alexandra Palace closed completely.

1946 (A3407)

Barking

Barking was and is an important junction on the erstwhile London, Tilbury & Southend Railway and is also served by the District Line of London Underground. This view, taken looking northeastwards, show the eight platform faces of the station. The railway first reached Barking on 13 April 1854 with the opening of the line from Forest Gate to Tilbury Fort via Dagenham; the line was jointly promoted by the Eastern Counties and the London & Blackwall railways. Barking became a junction once the cut-off route to Gas Factory Junction (at Bow) was opened on 31 March 1857. This line had been authorised on 7 July 1856. From the date of its opening, trains to Southend operated to Fenchurch Street, although the Eastern Counties (late the GER) continued to run from Barking to Bishopsgate until 1918. The somewhat complex ownership of the line was eventually to be regularised as the LT&SR, following the company's inability to persuade the GER to operate the route, started to operate the line itself in the mid-1870s. A further cut-off route, running via Upminster from Barking Tilbury Line Junction East was authorised on 24 July 1882 and opened on 1 June 1888. The line was quadrupled eastwards to Barking in the first decade of the 20th century, the section between East Ham and Barking being completed in 1908. This allowed for the introduction of District Railway services to the station, these commencing to Barking on 1 April 1908. The District trains were electric-operated and used the northernmost pair of lines into the station. The LT&S was to become part of the Midland Railway on 1 January 1912. The photograph shows Barking in 1931, immediately before the quadrupling of the line towards Upminster, which was opened on 12 September 1932 and allowed for the extension of District line services eastwards. Note on the road bridge — a level crossing until 1907 — in front of the main station building, the electric tram. Pictured in the days before the creation of the London Passenger Transport Board, this is operating over section of tramway controlled by Barking Urban District Council. These were converted to trolleybus operation in the late 1930s. The station itself was also remodelled in the 1930s. Today, Barking sees District Line services running to and from Upminster whilst the majority of main line passenger services through the station are in the hands of c2c although the solid diet of EMUs represented by that company's services to and from Fenchurch Street is, to an extent, relieved by the DMU shuttle operated by Silverlink to Gospel Oak. Initial electric services were introduced through Barking on 6 November 1961 and a full timetable commenced on 18 June 1962.

9 September 1931 (36591)

Barking

These two photographs, taken from the northwest, show the approaches to Barking and the complex junction that exists between the District/Metropolitan and ex-LTS line from Fenchurch Street with the line from Barking towards Woodgrange Park. The scene as illustrated here was largely the result of work undertaken in connection with the electrifcation of the ex-LTS lines. The new station, formally opened on 29 September 1961, was associated with the construction of a modified junction, including flyovers and underpasses, designed to eliminate conflicting movements. Dominating the left hand photograph is the East Ham depot used to house the EMUs that serve the ex-LTS lines out of Fenchurch Street; it is located between the up and down LTS lines. Alongside the down LTS line, to the north of the depot, are the two lines of the District/Metropolitan Line. From the north can be seen the line coming from Woodgrange Park. In the foreground, made evident by the curve of the housing, is the route of the spur from East Ham Loop South Junction to East Ham Loop North Junction; this opened in 1894 and was to close completely on 15 September 1958. The second photograph (inset) shows in more detail the complex junction arrangement immediately to the west of Barking station, with the station itself towards the top right of the photograph. Also visible in the left foreground is the freight spur into the Barking Trust Estates. For an account of the development of the railways in Barking, please see p14.

27 August 1961 (A94777/A94780)

Barnes Bridge

A site familiar to countless millions courtesy of the
annual Oxford-Cambridge boat race, Barnes Bridge is
the point at which the ex-LSWR Hounslow loop crosses
the River Thames. Immediately to the south of the river
is Barnes Bridge station itself with the three-arch bridge
linking the Middlesex and Surrey banks of the river.
The Hounslow Loop was authorised as part of the
1847 Act that permitted the construction of the line
through Richmond to Windsor. The line opened from
Barnes to Isleworth on 22 August 1849, although
Barnes Bridge station itself did not open until 12 March
1916, and thence to Feltham Junction on the following
1 February. The final part of the triangular junction at
Whitton was opened on 1 January 1853. The Hounslow
Loop continues to provide, as it has always done, a local
passenger service, services which are today in the hands
of SouthWest Trains.

26 November 1965 (A155765)

Battersea

Viewed from the northwest, the stark lines of Battersea Power Station dominates this view of the south bank of the Thames. Designed by Giles Gilbert Scott — famous also as the architect of Liverpool Anglican cathedral and the original phonebox — Battersea Power Station was constructed in the 1930s; it had a life of some 50 years before being closed in the 1980s. Unlike another of Scott's Thames-side power stations — Bank — which found a ready reuse as a museum — Tate Modern — when it closed, there has been considerable uncertainty as to the future of Battersea Power Station since it closed. Almost 20 years after it ceased to generate power, the building stands in a near derelict condition, open to the elements, although work is to start shortly on converting the building into flats. The origins of Victoria station, situated on the north bank of the Thames at this point, and of the approaches across the river date to the 1850s when the London, Chatham & Dover and London, Brighton & South Coast railways jointly promoted the Victoria Station & Pimlico Railway, which was incorporated in 1858. The LBSCR platforms were opened on 1 October 1860; these were used by the LCDR from 3 December 1860 until its own platforms were opened on 25 August 1862. As the GWR had running powers into the station — indeed was a part owner of the station until 1932 — some of the LCDR track was dual gauge in order to accommodate the GWR's broad gauge trains from Southall. The station was considerably expanded prior to World War 1, the LBSCR section being completed in 1908 and the SECR — as the LCDR had become — in 1909. The freight yards on the south bank of the Thames have closed — for example, Battersea Wharf lost its freight facilities on 4 May 1970.

12 May 1958 (A70754)

Beckenham Junction

Pictured looking towards the west, Beckenham Junction station can be seen astride the line between Herne Hill and Shortlands. The first line to reach the future Beckenham Junction — then known simply as Beckenham — was the Mid-Kent Railway — later South Eastern Railway — line from Lewisham which opened on 1 January 1857 and which terminated at Beckenham. The station became a junction the following year with the opening of the line from Bromley Bow Junction, to the north of Norwood Junction, to Bickley on 3 May 1858. Electric services over the Herne Hill-Shortlands section commenced on 12 July 1925 and over the original route towards Lewisham on 28 February 1926. The line from Penge Junction, slightly to the west of Beckenham Junction, to Herne Hill opened in 1863. As illustrated in this view, Beckenham Junction was provided with through platforms on the up and down line and bay platforms at the western end, on the up side, for the line towards Crystal Palace and, on the down side, for the line towards Lewisham. When recorded in 1970 there was also a coal concentration depot on the down side; this has subsequently closed and the site used for a Waitrose supermarket. The curve towards Lewisham was singled in 1987. More recently the line towards Crystal Palace has also been singled in order to incorporate the single line of the Croydon Tramlink that terminates alongside the bay platform on the up side.

14 August 1970 (A206828)

Bishopsgate

With the station throat at Liverpool Street in foreground, with the presence of modern traction evident, and with the ex-North London Railway line to Dalston Junction heading through Shoreditch station (closed on 4 October 1940) on the left, the major freight depot at Bishopsgate dominates the centre of this view taken in the early 1960s. The first railway to serve Bishopsgate — then called Shoreditch (it was renamed on 27 July 1846) — was the Eastern Counties Railway, which extended its line from Mile End on 1 July 1840. It was to be the GER's terminus until the first part of Liverpool Street, serving suburban services, opened on 2 February 1874; low-level platforms at Bishopsgate opened at the same time. Final closure to passenger services occurred on 1 November 1875 with the opening of the remainder of Liverpool Street station. At this date, the low level station lost its suffix, becoming known simply as 'Bishopsgate' until closure on 22 May 1916. The station was reopened as a goods yard on 1 January 1881 and was to survive in use until destroyed by fire on 5 December 1964; the scale of activity even as late as 1963 is evident in this photograph. Following the fire, the site stood derelict for some 40 years but is currently being integrated into the scheme for the extension of the East London Line to Dalston. Broad Street was the terminus of the North London Railway and opened to passenger traffic on 1 November 1865 and to freight on 18 May 1868. The NLR's goods yard was located to the north of the passenger station. Passenger services into Broad Street were converted to electric operation on 1 October 1916. Freight facilities at Broad Street were withdrawn on 27 June 1969 and passenger services reduced to peak hours only in May 1985 although final passenger services were not withdrawn until 30 June 1986.

8 May 1963 (A110906)

Blackfriars

With the platforms of Ludgate Hill station, which was opened initially as a temporary station on 21 December 1864 and as a permanent station on 1 June 1865 and had closed on 3 March 1929, in the foreground this view shows Blackfriars station on the north bank of the River Thames with the ex-South Eastern & Chatham Railway lines towards London Bridge and Herne Hill heading southwards. The first of the railway bridges at Blackfriars opened on 1 June 1864 although initially the passenger terminus was on the southbank of the river. This lasted only six months and, on closure, became part of the goods depot visible across the river; this depot closed in 1965. Ludgate Hill station was originally provided with two island platforms, it was modified, as shown here, to a single island platform in 1910. On 10 May 1886 a parallel bridge across the river was opened to serve a new station which was named St Pauls; this name was changed to Blackfriars on 1 February 1937 in order to avoid confusion with the new London Transport station of the same name. Blackfriars station suffered considerably during the war but was repaired; it underwent a major reconstruction between 1973 and 1977. In 1985 the original 1864 bridge across the river was dismantled, leaving the newer bridge to carry all traffic.

27 April 1961 (A86875)

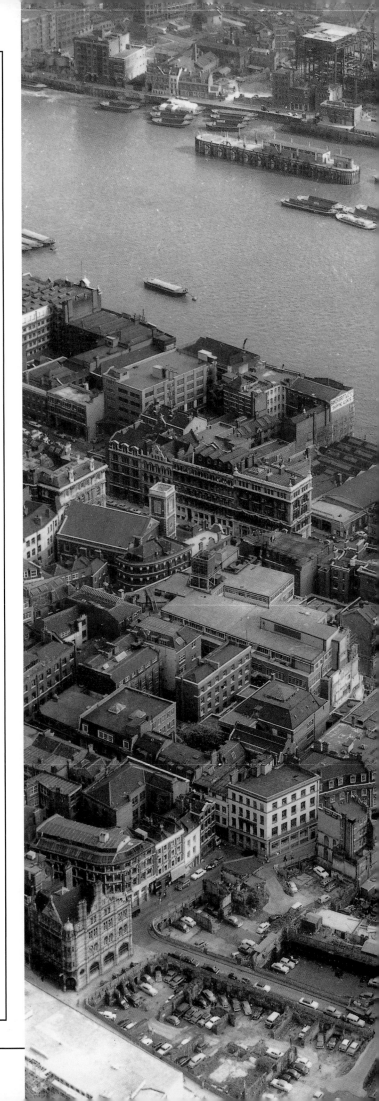

Blackfriars/Holborn Viaduct

In the foreground can be seen Blackfriars station; known originally as St Pauls when it first opened on 10 May 1886, the station was renamed on 1 February 1937 to avoid confusion with the new station recently opened on LT's Central Line. The first bridge across the river at this point was opened in 1864 and served Ludgate Hill station; this station was closed on 3 March 1929 but at this date still retained its platform awnings. It is interesting to compare this view with that taken looking southwards four years later (see p26) as, during the period, the awnings have been dismantled. In the centre of the photograph can be seen the platforms of Holborn Viaduct station. The through line from Ludgate Hill to Farringdon was opened to passenger services on 1 January 1866 and the new terminus at Holborn Viaduct, designed to relieve pressure at Ludgate Hill, opened on 2 March 1874; a second station, called Snow Hill, was opened adjacent to Holborn Viaduct on the through lines on 1 August 1874. This station was renamed Holborn Viaduct (Low Level) in 1912 and was to lose its passenger services in 1916. The short section of line between Ludgate Hill Junction and Farringdon was to close completely but was to be reopened with the completion of the Thameslink project in 1990. Holborn Viaduct station as illustrated here was destined to be rebuilt between 1960 and 1963 but was to close on 29 January 1990 with the reopening of the line to Farringdon and be replaced by new platforms on the lower level. Today the station is called City Thameslink.

12 June 1957 (A67557)

Brentford (GWR)

The once extensive facilities provided by the Great Western Railway are clearly demonstrated in this view of the branch heading northwards. Four miles long, the branch was built as a broad gauge line by the Great Western & Brentford Railway, a company incorporated on 14 August 1855. The line opened for freight traffic on 18 July 1859 and to passenger traffic on 1 May 1860. The passenger station was located slightly to the north of this view. The line was leased to the GWR in 1859 and taken over on 1 January 1872. The line was originally single track, but a standard gauge line was added in October 1861; the remaining broad gauge track was converted to standard gauge in 1876. Always the poor relation of the LSWR station in the town, passenger services over the GWR branch were withdrawn on 4 May 1942. Closure of the dock, on 31 December 1964, threatened the line's future and resulted in the closure of the section illustrated here, with the branch now terminating at the site of the old Brentford Town (GWR) station. Initially, the line northwards was retained for freight traffic from the various industrial concerns located along the Great West Road but, more recently, refuse trains running from Brentford to Didcot have provided the primary source of traffic.

6 October 1964 (A141293)

Brentford (LSWR)

With Brentford FC's Griffin Park football ground in the foreground, this view, taken looking towards the northeast, shows the approaches to and the triangle at Kew Bridge. Visible between the triangle and the River Thames is one of the water pumping stations, a location now well known to many as the home of the Kew Bridge steam museum. The LSWR Hounslow Loop was authorised to the Windsor, Staines & South Western Railway in 1847 and was opened from Barnes, through Brentford, to Isleworth on 22 August 1849. It was extended to Feltham Junction, on the Richmond-Staines line on 1 February 1850. The curve from Hounslow to Whitton was not opened until 1 January 1883. The North & South Western Junction Railway was authorised in 1851 to construct the line from Old Kew Junction, to the west of Kew Bridge station, to Willesden. Freight traffic over the line commenced on 15 February 1853 and, on 1 August 1853, passenger services operated by the North London Railway commenced. These initially ran to Twickenham but, from 1863, were extended to Kingston. On 1 February 1863 a curve facing eastwards to New Kew Junction was opened along with Kew Bridge station with its platforms on both the LSWR and NLR routes. The importance of the NLR line to Kew diminished with the opening of the Acton-Richmond line on 1 January 1869, after which date half the NLR services ran over the new route and the remainder continued to Kew Bridge. The LSWR services were electrified on 12 March 1916 and the NLR route to Kew Bridge followed, along with the rest of the line, on 1 October 1916. Passenger services over the NLR section to Kew Bridge were withdrawn on 12 September 1940. More recently, for a brief period, a service operated between Basingstoke and East Anglia over the Hounslow Loop and over the ex-NLR line towards Willesden.

1 July 1957 (A68141)

Bricklayers Arms

It was the South Eastern Railway that, faced with excessive charges to use London Bridge station, decided to build its own independent terminus at Bricklayers Arms. Built on a site selected by Sir William Cubitt, the SER's engineer, the new station opened on 1 May 1844. However, it was inconveniently located with the result that it never thrived as a passenger station and regular passenger services ceased in January 1852. The station was converted into a goods yard and this was further expanded by the opening of the adjacent London, Brighton & South Coast Railway goods yard — Willow Walk. The two yards were united by the SR under the name Bricklayers Arms on 7 March 1932. Also visible, located between the SER goods shed and the LBSCR yard, are the various elements of Bricklayers Arms shed. Immediately to the north of Willow Walk yard is the so-called 'New Shed'; this was built by the SER in 1869 and modified in 1938. This structure was severely damaged during the war, when it lost its roof, and was used for storage of locomotives. 'St Patricks Shed' was converted from a carriage shed in 1902 and was reroofed in 1937. The second shed at Bricklayers Arms was constructed in 1847; an earlier shed had been built in 1844, but had been demolished in 1869. The 1847-built shed was again reroofed by the Southern Railway in 1937. Coded 73B by British Railways, Bricklayers Arms closed on 17 June 1962. Although a centralised parcels depot was established on the site in 1969, conventional freight traffic declined. The line was to be closed completely on 7 October 1983.

31 July 1957 (68614)

Bromley North

The 1.75-mile long Bromley North branch from Grove Park, promoted by the Bromley District Railway, opened on 1 January 1878 and was taken over by the South Eastern Railway the following year. The branch terminus as illustrated here in the late 1920s was the result of rebuilding in 1925 in connection with the electrification of the branch. The original station had been provided with two platforms and three running lines, the latter terminating in a turntable. The new station was provided with a single two-sided platform of 520ft in length. Electric services were inaugurated along the branch on 28 February 1926. Alongside the passenger station is the small goods yard provided at the station; this was to close on 20 May 1968. Today, Bromley is still served by EMUs; these are now operated by the South Eastern TOC franchisee.

10 August 1929 (28346)

Bromley South

Viewed looking towards the east, Bromley South is one of the main intermediate stations on the ex-SECR line from Victoria to Orpington via Beckenham and Shortlands. The line through Bromley was promoted by the Mid-Kent Railway and the station at Bromley opened on 22 November 1858. Originally known as simply Bromley, the station was also briefly known as Bromley Common; it became Bromley South with the opening of the Bromley North branch in 1878. The station as illustrated in this 1964 view was the result of the reconstruction in connection with the 1959 scheme for the electrification of Kent Coast services. Suburban electric services through Bromley South commenced on 12 July 1925 but was it was not until 18 June 1962 that the second phase of the Kent Coast scheme saw long-distance services to Maidstone, Dover and Ramsgate converted.

13 March 1964 (A124078)

Burnt Oak

The penultimate station on the Northern Line extension from Golders Green to Edgware, Burnt Oak was opened with the section from Hendon to Edgware on 18 August 1924. This photograph, although undated, was taken within a decade of the line's opening and shows well the extent of housing development that had occurred by the 1930s.

1930 (31583)

Camden

Dating to April 1920, this is the oldest photograph to feature in this book. Pictured towards the northeast, the photograph records the approaches to Euston station in the period immediately prior to the Grouping of the railways when the LNWR was still very much the 'Premier Line'. In the centre of the foreground can be seen the platforms of Chalk Farm station; this had originally opened in 1851 but by the date of the photograph had already been closed (in 1917) and from the photograph would appear to be in the process of being demolished. Immediately to the east of the station can be seen the roundhouse that represented the second engine shed constructed by the LNWR at this point. Originally built in 1847 and known as the 'Luggage Engine House', this shed was closed in 1871 and leased out. The building still survives and is now listed. It is currently undergoing a major refurbishment, having been an arts centre for many years. Also originally built in 1847 and known as the 'Passenger Engine House', the five-road shed that was still operational in 1920 can be seen to the south of the station in the extreme right of the photograph. This structure was to be extended and reroofed by the LMS and was to survive until closure on 9 September 1963. The shed was subsequently demolished with the site utilised for sidings.

April 1920 (804)

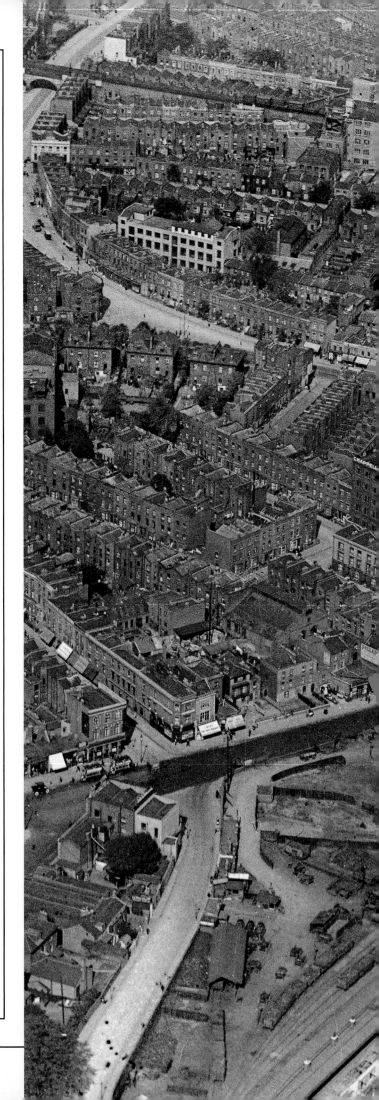

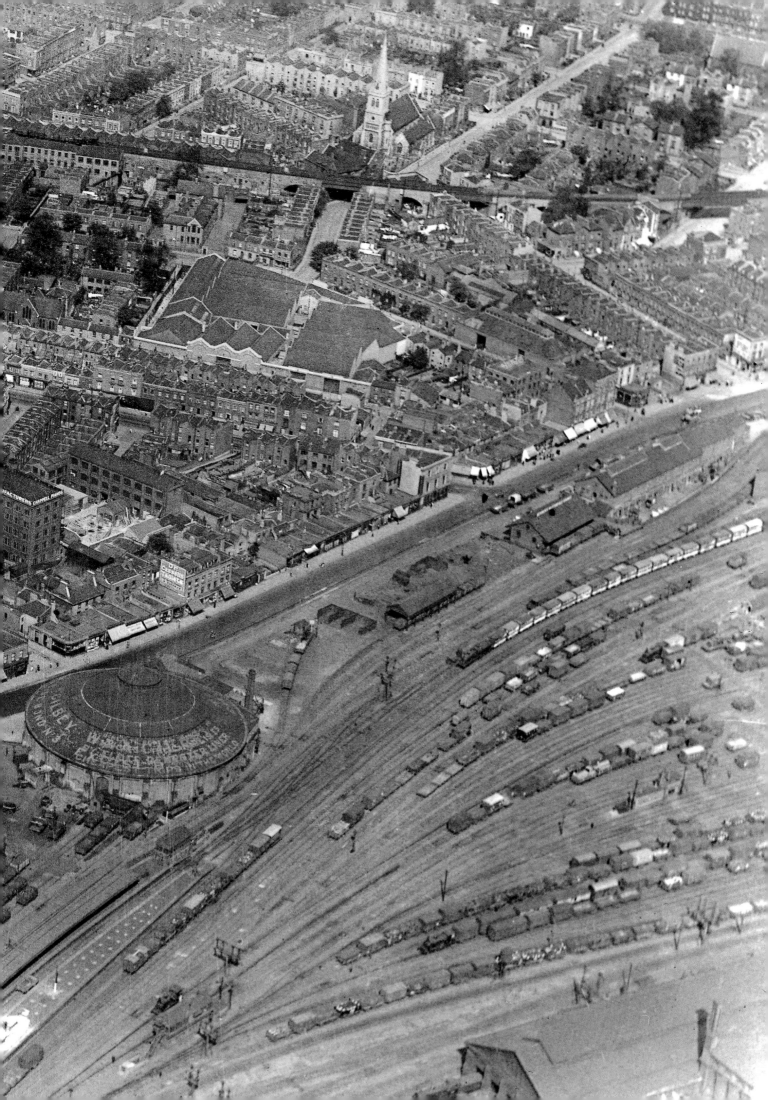

Camden Road

With Primrose Hill goods depot, on the West Coast main line in the distance, this view taken looking westwards shows Camden Road station in the centre. Immediately to the west of the station is Camden Road Junction; the line to the north heads towards Gospel Oak whilst that to the west connects to the main line out of Euston. The North London line from the east opened as far as Camden Road — known as Camden Town from 1870 to 1950 — on 7 December 1850 and thence to Primrose Hill (or Hampstead Road as it was then known) on 9 June 1851. Originally built as double track the route east of Camden Town (as it was then known) was quadrupled in 1871 as far as Dalston and thence to Broad Street four years later. The route north via Gospel Oak to Willesden was promoted as the Hampstead Junction Railway in order to alleviate congestion on the route north from Hampstead Road and opened on 2 January 1860. Although owned by the London & North Western Railway, services were provided by the North London Railway. The North London Line from Richmond via Camden Town to Broad Street was electrified from 1 October 1916 with the section from Camden Town to Primrose Hill following on 30 October 1922 as part of the scheme to electrify the suburban services from Euston to Watford.

26 October 1969 (A200585)

Cannon Street

One of a number of London termini that served the Southern Region and its antecedents, Cannon Street owes its origins to the South Eastern Railway, which opened the station on 1 September 1866. The station was built on a viaduct some 700ft in length; the viaduct required some 27m bricks for its construction. The station facade was represented by a five-storey hotel designed by E. M. Barry. This was originally known as the City Terminus Hotel but was renamed Cannon Street Hotel in 1879. The roof of the hotel can be seen in the photograph behind the dramatic trainshed, designed by Sir John Hackshaw, of the station itself. The photograph was taken in 1936, shortly after the introduction of suburban electrification had led to the wholesale remodelling of track at Cannon Street. This had taken place between 5 June and 28 June 1926 and had involved the temporary closure of the station for the duration. The station was severely damaged by wartime bombing; the hotel (which, by that time had been converted to offices) was to close permanently as a result of Blitz damage in 1941 and the trainshed was also to suffer severely and be subsequently demolished.
Today Cannon Street remains a major terminal for services provided by the Train Operating Company that serves Kent; although the towers at the southern end of the station remain to remind passengers of the once grand train shed that stood on the site, wholesale redevelopment of the area has altered the station.

17 June 1936 (PM1778)

Caterham

The almost irresistible rise of the dormitory town in southeast England is perhaps well exemplified by Caterham, which developed rapidly from the mid-19th century once the branch towards Purley was opened. Promoted by the Caterham Railway (which had been incorporated in 1854), the line was completed by 21 September 1855. However, due to a dispute between the Caterham Railway and both the London, Brighton & South Coast and South Eastern railways, the line did not actually open until 4 August 1856, with normal services commencing the following day. Initially, the Caterham Railway operated its own services, but in July 1859 it went bankrupt and was taken over by the SER. The route was originally constructed single-track, but was doubled in 1897 and the station illustrated here was the result of a SER replacement in 1900, when the original station closed. The line was electrified during the expansion of the Southern Railway's electrified network during the 1920s, with services commencing on 25 March 1928. At the time of the aerial photograph, Caterham was still provided with freight facilities; these were, however, to be withdrawn on 28 September 1964.

23 October 1952 (A47572)

Charing Cross

Viewed from the north and with the hotel prominent, Charing Cross station owes its origins to the South Eastern Railway, which promoted a line from London bridge, via Waterloo, across the river. Work started in 1862 and the first trains operated into the new station on 11 January 1864. The overall trainshed roof illustrated here was constructed after the original roof, designed by Sir John Hackshow, collapsed on 5 December 1905. Although the collapse was relatively slow, allowing for the removal of all trains and the evacuation of the station, six people were unfortunately killed. Charing Cross remains an essential London terminus today, although the trainshed roof has been replaced by the construction of an office block and, alongside the railway bridge, the original pedestrian Hungerford Bridge has been replaced by two new footbridges, one on either side of the railway bridge. The 250-bed hotel, however, remains although the forecourt is now enclosed by a fence and gates.

23 June 1962 (A103459)

Chelsea Basin

With Lots Road power station dominating the centre of this view, Chelsea Basin, with its extensive sidings, can be seen on the north bank of the Thames. Work started on the construction of Lots Road in March 1902 and it first opened on 1 February 1905 although not reaching full design capacity until 1908 (although it was later expanded); designed to power the electrified tube lines, it had a life of an almost exactly a century before being finally closed in 2005. The West London Extension Railway was extended south from Kensington Canal basin over Cremorne Bridge to Clapham Junction on 2 March 1863. Chelsea Basin opened contemporaneously with the line. In this view, taken in the mid-1960s, there is still considerable freight traffic evident; to the west of the basin can be seen the running lines heading north-south. Chelsea Basin was to close in 1981 and the site has been subsequently redeveloped, as has the site on the western side of the railway, as residential accommodation, bringing a significant number of residents to this once highly-industrial area. Reflecting the changing patterns of metropolitan life, a new passenger station, called Imperial Wharf, is planned for opening at the point where the Chelsea Basin lines diverged later in 2006.

26 November 1965 (A155803)

Chingford

Chingford, seen here in 1972, was first served by a branch of the Great Eastern Railway, which opened on 17 November 1873. The original line was single track but the route was doubled in September 1878 when the line was extended north by a mile to the terminus illustrated here. The original station then became a goods yard, surviving until the withdrawal of freight facilities on 4 October 1965. The Chingford line was one of those Liverpool Street services electrified at 6.2kV with electric services being introduced on 21 November 1960. The line was converted to 25kV in 1983.

13 July 1972 (A233834)

Clapham Junction

Now proudly boasting itself to be Britain's busiest railway station, Clapham Junction station did not open until 2 March 1863, some 25 years after the opening of the London & Southampton Railway from Nine Elms to Woking on 21 May 1838 had first brought the railways to the district. The location became a junction, albeit still without a station, when the Richmond Railway, authorised by an act of 21 July 1845, opened its line west towards Putney on 27 July 1846. The next arrival was the West End of London & Crystal Palace Railway, later to become part of the LBSCR, which was authorised on 4 August 1853, to construct a line from Crystal Palace to the south bank of the Thames; this line was opened between Wandsworth Common and Pimlico (as the south bank station was known) on 29 March 1858. However, it was the arrival of a fourth railway — the West London Extension Railway — on 2 March 1863 that resulted in the necessity for opening the new station. Jointly controlled by the LNWR and GWR, this new line provided a link, via Kensington, to the main lines from Paddington and Euston. Over the years, the station has expanded considerably (most notably during the early years of the 20th century), resulting in, at its peak, no fewer than 17 platforms, although only 16 remain in use today with No 1 being now trackless and No 2 used solely for the Silverlink Metro service to Willesden Junction. Also visible in this view looking towards the northwest is the massive Clapham Junction A signalbox that straddles the ex-LSWR lines on the east of the station and, located at the bottom right of the photograph, the Victoria Signalling Centre.

26 November 1965 (A155788)

Cricklewood

Looking northwest along the Midland Railway main line towards Bedford and with the station visible in the foreground, the extensive facilities provided at Cricklewood in the mid-1950s are readily apparent in this view. The MR originally reached London via the Great Northern Railway courtesy of a link between Bedford and Hitchin, but opened its own line to the Metropolis on 8 September 1867 for freight and to passenger services on 23 July 1868. The station, known originally as Childs Hill & Cricklewood, opened on 2 May 1870 being renamed in 1903. From Brent Curve Junction, through Dudding Hill Junction, to the southwest a link was opened on 1 October 1868 towards Willesden; the location became a triangle when the line from Cricklewood Curve Junction, just north of the station, to Dudding Hill Junction opened in 1870. Between 1875 and 1902 the lines towards Willesden carried a passenger service. Immediately to the east of the station are the carriage sidings. Beyond Cricklewood Curve Junction, on the down side, are the Cricklewood Recess Sidings and, immediately to the north of Brent North Junction, again on the down side, Cricklewood engine shed can be seen. The engine shed here was originally opened in 1882 and extended the following year; by the date of this photograph both parts of the shed had been reroofed by BR (in 1949). The shed was to close on 14 December 1964 and, after a brief period as a diesel stabling point, was demolished. Today Cricklewood is a pale shadow of its former self, although both the main line and the route to Willesden remain open. The passenger lines have been electrified, but much of the old railway land has either been redeveloped or left derelict. The sidings on the down side are still extant but the EMU depot constructed as part of the suburban electrification is closed.

1 June 1955 (A59184)

Crystal Palace

Photographed shortly after the end of World War 2, Crystal Palace (Low Level) is situated to the south of the building from which it took its name, which had been largely obliterated by fire more than a decade previously. The site, with the remains of Joseph Paxton's massive building can be seen between the station and Crystal Palace Parade, the road towards the north of the site. The Crystal Palace was originally constructed for the Great Exhibition of 1851 and located in Hyde Park; after the exhibition closed, the building was dismantled and relocated to the site near Sydenham. Promoted by the London, Brighton & South Coast Railway, the West End of London & Crystal Palace Railway was authorised to construct a 5.75-mile long line from Sydenham, past the site of the reconstructed Crystal Palace, to Wandsworth and the River Thames; the scheme was part of the LBSCR's plans for its own London terminus, plan which culminated in the construction of Victoria station (see p232). The line opened on 1 December 1856 and Crystal Palace became a junction station with the opening of the line to Norwood Junction on 1 October 1857. Electric services first reached Crystal Palace when the line from Victoria to the station was inaugurated on 12 May 1911; they were extended to Norwood Junction on 1 June 1912. The lines were originally fitted with catenary but this was replaced by the third rail in the early 1920s.

1 May 1950 (R7888)

Crystal Palace

There was a second line to serve Crystal Palace; this was the South Eastern Railway branch from Peckham Rye, authorised on 17 July 1862 as the Crystal Palace & South London Junction Railway and opened in 1865. The branch was electrified from 12 July 1925. At the date of the photograph, 1952, the ex-SER branch still retained passenger services but these were withdrawn on 20 September 1954 at which time the line beyond Nunhead was closed completely. This view, taken looking towards the north, shows the line running from the substantial station buildings provided towards Paxton Tunnel. In terms of a cross-reference to the photograph of Crystal Palace (Low Level), the water towers and reservoirs alongside Crystal Palace Parade can be seen top left in the Low Level photograph (see page 60).

14 March 1952 (A41940)

Docklands Light Railway

With the rise of container traffic and the decline of traditional methods of handling goods at ports, there was a shift of maritime traffic away from London's historic docklands. As a result, there was the opportunity for massive economic regeneration and redevelopment in this area; however, before such development could occur, there also needed to be a considerable improvement in public transport provision for an area that was almost devoid of passenger railways by this date. The result of this much needed investment was the Docklands Light Railway and these three photographs illustrate aspects of the DLR relatively early in its career; indeed, although these photographs are less than 20 years old, they record scenes that are now as much history as some of those illustrations in this book from 80 years ago. As originally conceived, the DLR was to run from Tower Gateway to Poplar, where a triangular junction would allow services to head south to Island Gardens and north to Stratford. Also at Poplar would be the DLR's depot. The first of these three photographs (insert top) shows a panorama looking west with the depot in the foreground, the triangular junction in the centre and the lines heading south to Island Gardens and west into Central London; expansion of the DLR, particularly with the eastward extension to Beckton, resulted in the radical reshaping of the junction at Poplar with the provision of flyovers to avoid conflicting movements. The second photograph (insert bottom) shows the original terminus at Island Gardens; this opened on 31 August 1987 with the rest of the original network but was to close in 1999 with the southern extension of the DLR to Lewisham via Greenwich. The third (main) illustration shows more detail of the depot at Poplar with the Stratford line curving sharply to the north; again this area was remodelled for the opening of the Beckton extension in 1994.

11 June 1989 (558418/558414/558417)

Ealing Broadway

The important Underground terminus and interchange with the ex-GWR main line at Ealing Broadway is featured in this view looking towards the north. Visible in the station are both District and Central stock. Ealing, as it was then called, was one of the early stations on the Great Western Railway, opening in December 1838 shortly after the line itself. The District Railway arrived with the opening of its branch from Turnham Green on 1 June 1879; for a brief period between 1883 and 1885 District Railway services operated west of Ealing as far as Windsor. Electric services over the District Railway to Ealing commenced on 1 July 1905. Initial proposals for what eventually became the Central Line route to North Acton Junction and Shepherds Bush were made with the authorisation of the Ealing & Shepherds Bush Railway in 1905; these plans were later revised so that the new line would form an end-on junction with an extension of the Central London Railway. The route was opened for freight traffic on 16 April 1917 and to passenger services, electrified from the start, on 3 August 1920.

30 April 1952 (A42843)

Earls Court

With the Earls Court exhibition building dominating the photograph on the left-hand side, this view looking towards the south shows, in the distance, West Brompton station on the District Line; alongside can be seen the disused platforms on the West London Extension line. On the west of the line at West Brompton are the sidings associated with Brompton & Fulham Goods; this opened in 1892 and was to close in 1975. In the foreground, to the north of the A3218 road bridge, can be seen the Lillie Bridge depot of London Underground and, to its west, West Kensington Goods & Coal Yard; this opened in 1879 and was to close in 1975. Running to the north in this view are the lines leading towards Warwick Road Goods (opened in 1844 and closed in 1967), those of the West London Extension from Clapham Junction to Kensington and those of the District Line from Earls Court to Richmond and to Kensington. The first railway to serve the area was the West London Extension, which was opened from Kensington Canal basin to Clapham Junction on 2 March 1863; the original station at West Brompton opened three years later but was to be closed on 20 March 1940. The station was reopened on 30 May 1999. The District Railway link towards Earls Court opened on 12 April 1869; the line was extended to Putney Bridge on 1 March 1880. The extension of the District Railway from Earls Court to Hammersmith opened on 9 September 1874.

21 June 1963 (A114448)

East Croydon

Viewed looking towards the south, East Croydon station can be seen situated on the main line between Clapham Junction and Brighton. The town was an early recipient of the railways, as the Surrey Iron Railway linked Croydon with Wandsworth as early as 26 July 1803; the line was later extended to Merstham. The Croydon-Merstham section closed in 1838 and the original section in 1846. However, by that date, the London & Croydon Railway had arrived, opening on 1 August 1839 and the London & Brighton followed two years later; it is on the latter route that East Croydon is situated. The East Croydon station visible in this view dates back to its reconstruction in 1897/98; it was rebuilt in the early 1990's. Alongside, on the upside, is the extensive goods yard with plenty of traffic still in evidence. To the north of the station, an 0-6-0DM shunter can be seen shunting a rake of parcels wagons; despite all the traffic in this 1970 view, however, freight facilities were to be withdrawn from East Croydon in 1973. As is so often the case, the site of the goods yard is now used as a car park.

14 August 1970 (A206747)

East Finchley

Located on the ex-GNR 'Northern Heights' section of
the Northern Line, East Finchley is the point at which
the Northern Line reaches the surface on the Mill Hill
East/High Barnet section of the line. The line was
originally authorised on 3 June 1862 to provide a link
between Edgware and the GNR main line at Finsbury
Park. Initially promoted by an independent company,
but backed by the GNR and absorbed by it on 15 July
1867, the branch opened on 22 August 1867.
Originally built as single track, the line through East
Finchley was doubled in January 1870. Although
passenger services were extensive prior to World War 1,
postwar the situation deteriorated and, in 1935, plans
were developed for the transfer of the 'Northern Heights'
section from the LNER to the LPTB for electrification
and incorporation into the Northern Line. Following
work, the first Underground services reached East
Finchley on 3 July 1939, being extended to High Barnet
on 14 April 1940 and Mill Hill East on 18 May 1941;
the final steam-hauled passenger services through the
station ran on 2 March 1941. After the war, the
ambitious plans for the Edgware and Alexandra Palace
lines were not revived. LNER (and later BR) operated
freight services continued to serve Edgware via East
Finchley until mid-1964, at which date the physical
connection between East Finchley and Finsbury Park
was severed to the east of the depot constructed
alongside the ex-GNR route. This view shows the
station looking eastwards shortly before the final
withdrawal of the freight services.

9 October 1963 (A121756)

East Putney

With East Putney station in the foreground, the District Line from Wimbledon to Putney Bridge heads north-south. In the cutting can be seen the ex-LSWR Putney station, on the four-track section from Clapham Junction to Barnes, whilst from East Putney a curve heads to the east to connect with the Putney-Clapham Junction line at Point Pleasant Junction. The District Line section from Putney Bridge to East Putney opened on 3 June 1889. The LSWR route from Point Pleasant Junction to Wimbledon opened on the same day; the LSWR provided a service from Waterloo to Wimbledon via East Putney (with EMU operation from 25 October 1915 — the first LSWR service to be electrified), although this was suspended by the SR on 5 May 1941 and never reinstated. At Point Pleasant Junction, a flying junction was completed on 1 July 1889 (this was removed and the junction simplified a century later). The section south from Putney Bridge to Wimbledon was electrified from 27 August 1905. The LSWR route through Putney was authorised in 1847 and opened from Clapham Junction to Richmond on 22 August 1848. Electric services over the route commenced on 30 January 1916.

26 November 1965 (A155777)

Edgware

When the Edgeware (sic), Highgate & London Railway was incorporated on 3 June 1862, the route between Finsbury Park and the proposed terminus at Edgware was largely rural, with Finchley and Edgware having a combined population of less than 6,000 at the time of the 1861 census. However, travel from the area into London was difficult and the new railway promised to almost halve journey times between Edgware and London. The railway was promoted by the Great Northern Railway and absorbed by it on 15 July 1867, opening on the following 22 August. Until World War 1 services over the GNR's 'Northern Heights' routes were good but after the war a decline set in as a result of competition from tramways, buses and the Underground. In 1935 it was proposed that the Northern Heights lines be transferred to the LPTB and be converted to form part of an expanded Northern Line service. In order to facilitate the conversion passenger services over the ex-GNR branch to Edgware were suspended on 11 September 1939 and were never to resume. Whilst part of the conversion scheme was completed, war initially and then postwar austerity resulted in the scheme ultimately being left incomplete. Freight traffic continued to run from Edgware until official closure on 1 July 1964. This view of the ex-GNR station taken shortly after the opening of the Northern Line extension from Hendon shows to good effect the platform, extensive goods yard and the small locomotive servicing area. There had originally been a engine shed on the site, dating to the line's opening, but this had been closed in 1878 and destroyed a decade later.

30 June 1926 (15982 [C13371])

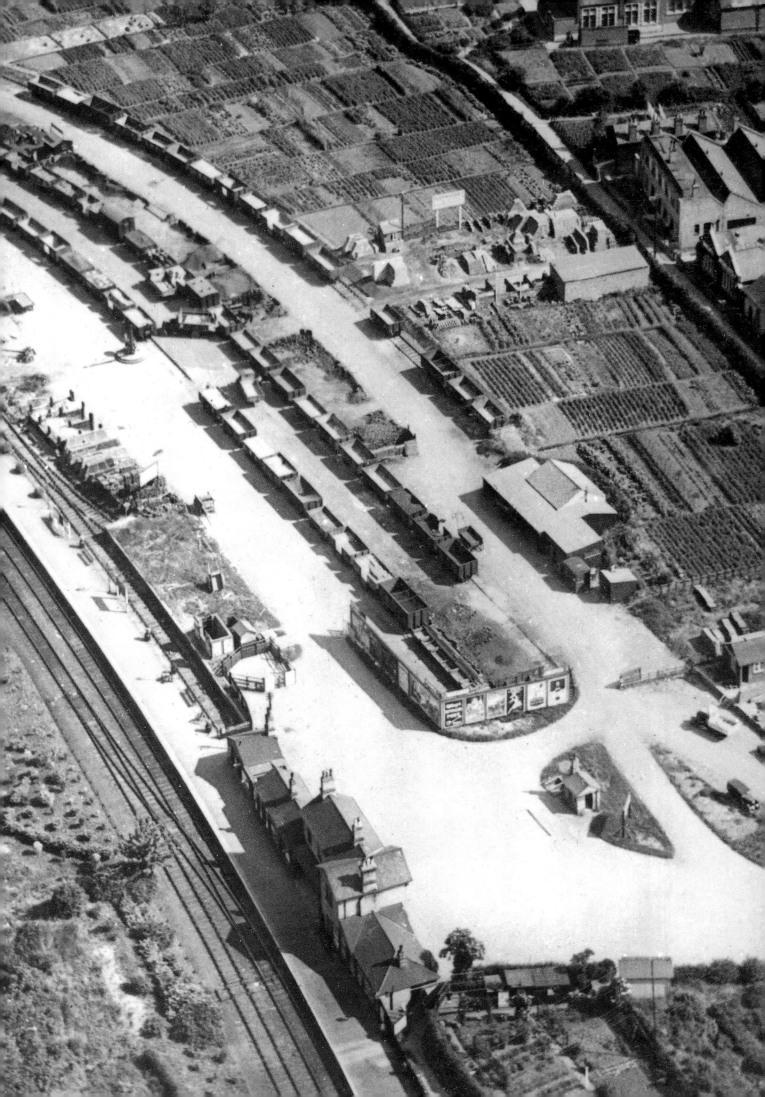

Edgware

Powers to extend the Hampstead Tube beyond Golders Green through Hendon to Edgware were obtained in 1902, before construction work on the Golders Green section had actually commenced, but it was to be some 20 years before the Underground finally reached the town. Work commenced on the extension in 1922 with the section from Golders Green to Hendon opening on 19 November 1923 and that from Hendon to Edgware on 18 August 1924. This view, taken some 18 months after the line's opening shows both how rural Edgware was at the time and also the route of the proposed extension of the line on towards Bushey. Edgware was designed as a through station and work in fact started in 1935 on the extension. World War 2, however, caused work to be suspended and it was never restarted with the result that Edgware remains one terminus of the Northern Line today. As with other Underground extensions, that to Edgware soon encouraged massive residential development and the quiet forecourt of the station evident in this view would also become the hub of a network of new bus routes radiating out to serve the new population.

27 may 1926 (15770)

Edgware

By July 1957, and some 30 years since the earlier views of Edgware, the massive growth in the town is all too evident in this view that shows the close proximity of the Northern Line station, on the left, and the ex-GNR station to the right. By this date the GNR station had lost its passenger services but was still served by freight trains from Finsbury Park; these would survive for a further seven years.

1 July 1957 (A68125)

Edmonton

Although much of the Aerofilms archive is taken from a relatively high level, there are still occasional photographs which allow for a closer examination of the locality — a case in point being this view of the Edmonton Empire and tramway terminus at Edmonton Town Hall. Visible in the background is the line that linked Lower Edmonton with Angel Road; this route had been opened on 1 March 1849 but had been largely superseded by the construction of the line from Stoke Newington to Lower Edmonton (High Level), which had opened on 22 July 1872. The original route retained limited passenger services until 11 September 1939 and was to close completely on 7 December 1964. The junction, and both Lower Edmonton stations, was to the left of the scene illustrated here. In the foreground can be seen the terminal stub provided by the Metropolitan Electric Tramways at this point with its scissors crossover. This was a short-working off the MET's main route northwards to Ponders End and Waltham Cross. Visible in the foreground is one of the MET's double-deck tramcars arriving at the terminus. The date of the photograph is significant; 27 June 1933 was within days of the creation of the LPTB at which stage MET would lose its independence. The MET was the largest of the three company fleets acquired by the LPTB on 1 July 1933, with a fleet totalling some 316 trams. The tram routes serving Edmonton were to be converted to trolleybus operation in 1938, the last to succumb being route 27 from Tottenham Court Road to Edmonton which was converted on 6 November of that year.

27 June 1933 (41999)

Enfield Chase

Viewed looking towards the north, Enfield Chase station is located to the west of Enfield Town station on the Hertford Loop line. The four mile branch from Wood Green — now called Alexandra Palace — to Enfield opened on 4 April 1871. The original terminus, by this date only a freight yard, can be seen to the left of the through station. This station was to close with the opening of the Hertford Loop line, designed by the GNR to provide additional capacity between Stevenage and Wood Green, between Grange Park and Cuffley on 4 April 1910. The line between Cuffley and Stevenage was opened as a single track on 4 March 1918 and doubled two years later. Freight facilities from the original station were withdrawn during 1974. The Hertford Loop continues in use, having been electrified in the 1970s, and retains its function as a diversionary route in the event of problems with the ECML south of Stevenage.

29 October 1928 (25291 [C13654])

Enfield Town

The branch to Enfield Town was opened from Angel Road, on the Tottenham Hale-Cheshunt route, to Enfield on 1 March 1849. With the opening of the line from Stoke Newington to Lower Edmonton on 22 July 1872 the original line from Edmonton to Angel Road became less significant although a few trains from Enfield Town continued to run via Angel Road until 11 September 1939. With the opening of the new route, the branch to Enfield Town was doubled and the original station rebuilt. Part of the original station, a 17th century house once used as a school, was preserved in the Victoria & Albert Museum on demolition. The new station was further expanded in 1902 through the construction of a third platform. By the date of the photograph the branch had been electrified as part of the programme of converting the suburban lines into Liverpool Street. Initially electrified at 6.25kV, public services with EMUs commenced over the branch on 21 November 1960. Conversion to 25kV took place in 1983.

28 May 1962 (A100163)

Epping

The Great Eastern Railway branch to Epping opened as far as Loughton on 22 August 1856 and this was to be the terminus of the line for a decade until it was extended through Epping to Ongar on 24 April 1865. The 11.5 mile extension was originally constructed as single track but the line was later doubled as far as Epping. The line passed from the GR to the LNER in 1923. In the mid-1930s proposals were made for the incorporation of the ex-GER branch and associated Fairlop Loop within an extended Central Line and for the route to be electrified. In the event, World War 2 intervened and the transfer and conversion did not take place until after the cessation of hostilities. Electric services were progressively extended along the line, with Loughton being reached on 21 November 1948. This was the terminus of electric services for less than a year before they were further extended to Epping on 25 September 1949. A steam shuttle continued to serve Ongar for a further decade, until electric services were introduced on 18 November 1957. This view, taking towards the north, shows the Central Line approach to Epping from the south shortly after the electrification of the line to Ongar. At this stage, steam-hauled freight services still operated; freight facilities at Epping were withdrawn in 1966. The extension of the line to Ongar was to be closed on 30 September 1994 although, more than a decade on, the line has reopened as a preservation scheme.

13 March 1964 (A124013)

Epsom

Viewed looking towards the north, this view of Epsom shows the station on the extreme left with the line heading towards Worcester Park heading towards the north and that towards Sutton heading to the northeast. The original LBSCR line to serve Epsom was that from Sutton; this opened on 10 May 1847 to a terminus located slightly to the east of the future junction. The original Epsom station — known latterly as Epsom Town — was to close on 3 March 1929 although it remained as a goods yard until final closure on 3 May 1965. The site of the original station can be seen towards the top right of the photograph. The LSWR arrived at the town courtesy of the Wimbledon & Dorking Railway; this was incorporated on 27 July 1857 and the line was opened, along with the new station at Epsom, on 4 April 1859. The section between Epsom and Leatherhead was jointly controlled by the LSWR and LBSCR with the latter extending its line to join the new route. The station as illustrated in this pre-World War 2 photograph was the result of rebuilding in 1929. Electric services over the route through Epsom from Raynes Park to Effingham Junction were introduced on 12 July 1925.

5 May 1938 (57023)

Euston

In the history of Britain's railways there have been few more controversial acts than the destruction of the Doric Arch at Euston as well as the demolition of the Great Hall. Swept away in the early 1960s, the loss of these structures was perhaps one of the defining moments in the conservation movement. Energising figures such as the late Poet Laureate, Sir John Betjeman, future campaigns to save, for example, Liverpool Street, proved more successful. This view, looking towards the north, shows to good effect the location of the Doric Arch and the sheer scale of Euston station as it existed in the late 1950s immediately prior to the massive redevelopment undertaken in connection with the electrification of the West Coast main line. The London & Birmingham Railway opened from Euston Square to Boxmoor on 20 July 1837, with services through to Birmingham opening on 17 September 1838. In both Birmingham and London, the railway marked its presence with a triumphal arch. Designed by Philip Hardwick, the arch has been called the 'finest classical monument in London'. The Great Hall and the rest of the building behind the arch, designed by Hardwick's son, was started in 1846 and thereafter the station grew dramatically so that prior to the demolition it comprised 15 platforms in all: Nos 1/2 (from 1873); No 3 (the original 1837 arrival platform); Nos 4/5 (of 1891); No 6 (the original 1837 departure platform); Nos 7/8 (short and rarely used); Nos 9/10 (dating from 1840) and 11 were used mainly for parcels; and, Nos 12-15 (dating from 1892 and, with a separate entrance, known as the West station) which were used for mainline services. Reconstruction of Euston had originally been proposed before the outbreak of World War 2, but work did not commence until 1963. The new station was formally opened on 14 October 1968.

20 June 1957 (A67809)

Fairlop

From the mid-19th century London's growth meant that significant population centres grew up in what had been previously rural Essex and, to cater for the growth in passenger traffic that resulted, the GER expanded its network of lines serving the region. Fairlop, pictured here viewed from the west shortly after the route was electrified was a loop line from a triangular junction on the Romford line to Woodford and was opened on 1 May 1903. From the mid-1930s proposals were made to incorporate the ex-GER lines to Epping and Ongar within an extended Central Line. Unfortunately, World War 2 intervened the conversion work was delayed until after the war. In order to further the conversion, steam-hauled passenger services over the Fairlop loop were withdrawn on 30 November 1947 and replaced by a temporary bus service. Electric services were extended as far north as Hainault on 31 May 1948 and via Fairlop itself to Woodford on 21 November 1948. BR continued to operate freight services over the line until the withdrawal of freight facilities; the small goods yard at Fairlop visible in this view was to close in 1958 although the final freight traffic over the route did not cease for a further seven years. Today Central Line trains continue to serve Fairlop station.

1954 (A55558/54)

Feltham

Located on the Richmond-Staines line, Feltham was one of the stations opened with the line on 22 August 1848. However, the location's importance grew with the development of the massive marshalling yard, which was developed progressively with the first phase opening on 3 October 1920. The concept, developed by Sir Herbert Walker, was to concentrate freight activities on a single location, streamlining work previously carried out at Nine Elms, Woking, Brentford, Brent and Willesden. Eventually the site was to occupy some 79 acres and, as shown in this view looking to the southwest, a locomotive shed. The shed was first opened in 1922 and was thus barely a decade old when recorded in this view. Primarily a base for freight locomotives, the facilities included a 65ft turntable, coaling stage and a two-track repair shed. The shed, which had an allocation of up to 80 locomotives, was to remain operational until final closure on 9 July 1967, with the end of SR steam, and was demolished subsequently. A small diesel depot was constructed where the coaling stage was located.
Also visible is the two-track wagon repair shed with the up marshalling sidings between it and the main line. In the background is Hanworth Airpark, where the *Graf Zeppelin* was displayed during its visit to the United Kingdom in July 1932. Feltham Yard was to close on 6 January 1969 and the site was largely derelict for some 30 years; more recently, the westernmost section has been redeveloped with a major Post Office facility occupying part of the site.

2 July 1932 (38819)

Fenchurch Street

The Aerofilms' archive includes both oblique and vertical photography; most of the images in this book are the former but it can sometimes be instructive to take the vertical view as in this case. One of the smallest of London's termini — it possesses only two platforms with four platform faces — Fenchurch Street can claim to be one of the oldest of the city's stations and also one with the most complex history. Its origins date back to the London & Blackwall Railway, whose line from Minories was extended into Fenchurch Street on 2 August 1841. The L&BR was initially cable operated, a means of propulsion that remained until 1849 when the trains operated by both the Eastern Counties and North London railways commenced operating into Fenchurch Street station. In order to accommodate the additional traffic, the route out to Stepney was widened in 1854 at which time the overall roof visible was constructed. The next arrival at the station was a company that, ultimately, was to dominate the scene — the London, Tilbury & Southend Railway (which was later to be taken over by the Midland Railway and subsequently form part of the LMSR). In 1865, North London Railway services were diverted to the new station at Broad Street. Also in 1865, the Great Eastern Railway took over the lease of the London & Blackwall; this was followed in 1874 by the opening of Liverpool Street station, which resulted in the majority of GER services being transferred to the new station. By the date of the photograph there had been considerable redevelopment around the station and this process has continued in the subsequent 40 years. Electric services — at (initially) 6.75kV — commenced on 6 November 1961 with the full timetable being introduced on 18 June 1962. Apart from electrification, the station has also seen the replacement of the overall roof by platform canopies but services still operate, now run by the successor of the LT&SR — the c2c franchise.

16 October 1968 (SV1368)

Finchley Central

Pictured looking towards the northeast, this view of
Finchley (Church End) — as it was then called; it only
became Finchley Central in 1940 — was taken shortly
before the Grouping of 1923 when the GNR 'Northern
Heights' lines passed to the LNER. The station was
originally opened with the opening of the single-track
branch from Finsbury Park to Edgware on 22 August
1867; the route was doubled as far as Finchley by
January 1870. The then named Finchley & Hendon
became a junction with the opening of the four-mile
branch to High Barnet on 1 April 1872. The branch
was also constructed as double track. By the mid-1930s,
steam services over the ex-GNR lines were increasingly
unreliable and, in 1935, a plan was formulated to
transfer the routes to the LPTB and electrify them as
part of an expanded Northern Line network. Northern
Line services started to operate to High Barnet on
14 April 1940 and, following a period when passenger
services were suspended after 11 September 1939 in
theory to permit doubling of the Edgware line, from
Finchley Central to Mill Hill East on 18 May 1941
over the extant single track. After the war, it was decided
in 1954 not to complete the conversion of the ex-GNR
routes, leaving Mill Hill East as the terminus of the short
spur from Finchley Central. Today, Northern Line trains
continue to operate through the station to both High
Barnet and Mill Hill East.

25 May 1921 (6286)

Finsbury Park

The ultimate station on the approach to King's Cross, Finsbury Park is the point at which the ex-GNR route towards Moorgate heads off to the southeast and, until it closed, was also the junction for the GNR branch towards Edgware and Alexandra Palace. This view, taken towards the west, shows the northern part of the station and the adjacent goods yard. Standing awaiting their next duty are two Type 2 (Class 31) diesels whilst in the foreground a southbound service towards King's Cross can be seen passing through the station. The station at Finsbury Park, originally called Seven Sisters Road, was opened initially on 1 July 1861, 11 years after the East Coast main line opened. The branch towards Edgware was opened on 22 August 1867, shortly before the station changed its name. The connection southeastwards to the North London Railway at Canonbury Junction followed in 1872 before the Great Northern & City line to Moorgate on 14 February 1904. The goods yard opened in 1865 and was to survive until freight facilities were withdrawn on 1 April 1968. Suburban services through Finsbury Park, including the line to Moorgate which had been closed between Finsbury Park and Drayton Park on 4 October 1964, were electrified in the early 1970s with services being introduced between 1976 and 1978; electrification north of Royston followed, with Peterborough being reached on 1 May 1987, and beyond. The inset photograph, taken at the same time as the main image, shows the southern half of the station and records the Type 2-hauled passenger service heading southwards to King's Cross. The train is approaching the junction with the line towards Canonbury Junction. Slightly further to the south, but out of view, was Finsbury Park depot; this was home to many of the 'Deltic' class locomotives used on ECML services. The depot is now closed and the site redeveloped for housing.

26 May 1963 (A112737/A112736)

Golders Green

One of the earliest photographs in the Aerofilms' archive is this dramatic view of Golders Green taken in April 1920, when the station seen here was the terminus of the Hampstead tube. Note the remarkable selection of buses parked on the station forecourt and, on the Finchley Road, a southbound open-top electric tramcar. The Hampstead Tube was authorised by an Act of 24 August 1893 but it was not until the first decade of the 20th century that progress was made. In 1901 Charles Tyson Yerkes acquired control through the Metropolitan District Electric Traction Co (the Underground Electric Railways Co from 1902) and, in September 1903, construction work started. The line opened from Charing Cross (then called Strand) to Golders Green on 23 January 1907. The opening of the railway was a major factor in the rapid development of the area, with massive residential development already evident by the date of this photograph. Also visible in the station is the depot used for the line's stock, which remains in use today. The line was extended beyond Golders Green to Hendon Central on 19 November 1923 and thence to Edgware on 18 August 1924, some 20 years after the line was originally authorised.

May 1920 (810)

Golders Green

It's less than a decade after the previous photograph of Golders Green but much has changed, most notably in the extension of the Northern line over the Finchley Road. The line was extended beyond from Golders Green to Hendon Central on 19 November 1923 and thence to Edgware on 18 August 1924, some 20 years after the line was originally authorised. On the roads, although there is a preponderance of open-top double-deck buses visible, it is also possible to see a covered-top bus in the station forecourt whilst a covered-top tram can also be seen, this time heading towards the north. This section of tramway was part of the Metropolitan Electric Tramways, which, like the Underground, would become part of the LPTB in 1933.

19 July 1929 (28190)

Grove Park

Located between Hither Green and Chislehurst, Grove Park station opened on 1 November 1871, some six years after the route through the area was opened. The line through Chislehurst was promoted by the South Eastern Railway as a means of shortening the route to Dover and was opened on 1 July 1865 as far as Chislehurst and thence to Tonbridge on 1 May 1868. The importance of Grove Park increased with the promotion of the 1.5-mile long branch to serve Bromley North. Promoted by the Bromley Direct Railway, the branch was opened on 1 January 1878 and taken over by the SER on 21 July 1879. This view taken looking towards the northeast shows clearly the main station building on Baring Road and the EMU sidings located on the down side. Slightly to the north of the station, just out of site on the left of the photograph, is the EMU depot.

18 August 1970 (A207309)

Gunnersbury

One of the two intermediate stations to the north of Richmond to be served by both District Line and North London Line services, Gunnersbury is the junction, visible at the bottom of this view looking towards the west, of the station taken in 1966. The line through Gunnersbury was originally constructed by the LSWR to linked Richmond with Addison Road (Kensington) and opened on 1 January 1869; simultaneously the North London Railway opened its line from South Acton Junction. The LSWR provided a connection with the District Line at Hammersmith, this being opened on 1 June 1877. Apart from LSWR and NLR services, four other companies, including the GWR and the MR, operated over the route into Richmond at various times, such was the importance of the location as a prosperous dormitory town. The District Railway services were electrified on 1 August 1905 and those of the North London Railway followed on 1 October 1916. LSWR services over the route were withdrawn on 3 June 1916, leaving the District and the North London Railway to operate the route alone. This view shows clearly the station's island platform and how hemmed in it is by more recent developments.

2 July 1966 (A164333)

Hackney Wick

With Victoria Park Junction in the foreground, this view towards the northwest shows the once extensive goods facilities at Hackney Wick between Stratford and Hackney Central. Although no evidence can be seen in this aerial view a passenger station called Victoria Park existed slightly to the west of the junction between 1856 and 1866 when it was relocated adjacent to the junction. Also called Victoria Park this new station closed in 1943. The North London Railway from Bow, via Victoria Park, to Islington opened on 26 September 1850. The Great Eastern line from Victoria Park to Stratford opened for freight on 15 August 1854 and to passenger services on 16 October the same year. By the date of the photograph, passenger services over both routes had ceased: the Great Eastern platforms at Victoria Park closed on 1 November 1942 and the North London service from Poplar to Dalston Junction was withdrawn on 15 May 1944 (although the NL platforms at Victoria Park had closed earlier, on 8 November 1943) albeit replaced by a substitute bus until 23 April 1945. Freight facilities were withdrawn from Hackney Wick on 6 November 1967. The line south from Victoria Dock Junction to Poplar Docks closed completely on 3 October 1983. Passenger services over the line from Dalston Junction to Stratford, through Hackney, were reinstated on 13 May 1985 as North London line services were gradually withdrawn from Broad Street station.

31 August 1961 (A96432)

Hadley Wood

This photograph shows an important transitional phase in the history of the railway at Hadley Wood in Hertfordshire, one of the suburban stations on the East Coast main line between Finsbury Park and Potters Bar. Although the Great Northern Railway opened its route north from London to Peterborough on 7 August 1850, it was not until 1 May 1885 that Hadley Wood station opened. The station is situated between Hadley Wood South Tunnel (384yd) and Hadley Wood North Tunnel (232yd). The photograph records work being undertaken in 1959 to quadruple the ex-GNR main line north from Finsbury Park. The work, as can be seen, included the construction of two new tunnels parallel to the existing structures as well as the building of a brand-new four-platform station. The work is well in hand by this date, but it is interesting to note that the original 1885 station building is still extant on the road over bridge.

The construction of the tunnels required the use of a special design of tunnelling shield, some 31ft in diameter, through which the London clay was excavated. In order to clear the spoil and transport the concrete sections require to line the tunnel a 2ft gauge railway was temporarily laid over the new formation. By the date of the photograph, all evidence of this had been removed. The new Hadley Wood tunnels were the first in Britain to be constructed using pre-cast concrete segments.

29 April 1959 (A74917)

Hainault

Viewed from the north, the massive Central Line depot dominates this view of the now-electrified Fairlop loop heading southwards. Beyond the depot can be seen Hainault station itself and in the distance the platforms of Fairlop itself. The Great Eastern Railway Fairlop loop was opened from a triangular junction on the Romford line to Woodford on 1 May 1903. From the mid-1930s proposals were made to incorporate the ex-GER lines to Epping and Ongar within an extended Central Line. In the event, World War 2 intervened and it was not possible to develop the plans until after the cessation of hostilities. In order to further the conversion, steam-hauled passenger services over the Fairlop loop were withdrawn on 30 November 1947 and replaced by a temporary bus service. Electric services were extended as far north as Hainault on 31 May 1948 and through to Woodford on 21 November 1948. BR-operated freight services continued to operate over the lines until the withdrawal of freight facilities from intermediate stations in 1965. Hainault depot comprises a running shed and sidings with, in the long building at the southern end of the site, a cleaning shed. The route remains open and still an integral part of the Central Line.

8 June 1962 (A103891)

Hammersmith

The complex network of lines that once served Hammersmith is clearly shown in this view looking towards the north. In the centre of the photograph is the Hammersmith & City terminus; this line, from Westbourne Park, was constructed as a broad gauge route and opened by the GWR on 13 June 1864. The line became jointly owned with the Metropolitan on 15 July 1867 with the Metropolitan operating passenger services. The line was converted to standard gauge in August 1868 and electrified from 5 November 1906. The line continues to operate today as part of the Underground network. On the right of the photograph is Hammersmith Broadway; this was reached by the District Railway on 9 September 1874 when the company opened its extension from Earl's Court. Further plans to extend westwards were ended by an agreement with the LSWR to allow running powers over the latter's route to Richmond. A connection from Hammersmith Broadway to the LSWR Richmond-Addison Road line at Studland Road Junction was opened on 1 June 1877. The LSWR route from Gunnersbury through to Addison Road opened on 1 January 1869 and a connection with the Hammersmith & City Railway at Grove Road Junction was opened on 1 June 1870. A station, called Grove Road, was located to the west of the H&C station on the ex-LSWR line. Passenger services were withdrawn over the Studland Road Junction-Addison Road section on 3 June 1916 and the line was to close completely at the same time. As can be seen in this post-World War 2 photograph, although the trackbed of the closed LSWR route is still readily identifiable, the track had been removed.

21 May 1949 (R10954)

Hampstead

An eight-car Metropolitan Line train heads east having just passed through West Hampstead with a service heading towards Baker Street. Running parallel to the north of the Metropolitan Line is the ex-MR main line from Cricklewood heading towards St Pancras with West Hampstead Midland — now West Hampstead Thameslink — station visible in the top left hand corner of the photograph. Passing over the ex-MR main line is the ex-North London line from Willesden to Gospel Oak; this also serves a station called West Hampstead, which is visible towards the centre left of the photograph. The first railway to serve Hampstead was the North London (albeit promoted by the LNWR as the Hampstead Junction Railway), which opened its route on 2 January 1860; it was not until 1888 that its station, then called West End Lane, opened. The Midland main line was the next arrival; this line was to open for freight between Bedford and London St Pancras on 8 September 1867 and to passenger services to Moorgate on 13 July 1868. Passenger services into St Pancras commenced on 1 October 1868. Again the station at West Hampstead, originally called West End (For Kilburn and Hampstead), post-dated the opening of the line, not being opened until 1871. The next line to be completed was the Metropolitan; this was opened from Swiss Cottage to West Hampstead on 30 June 1879 and from West Hampstead to Willesden Green on 24 November 1879. Running parallel with the Metropolitan Line is the ex-GCR main line into Marylebone; this was opened to freight on 27 July 1898 and to passenger services on the following 15 March. The final expansion occurred on 20 November 1939 when electrified Bakerloo Line services were extended north from Baker Street, over the Metropolitan Line metals, through West Hampstead towards Stanmore. At this date, Metropolitan Line services were also electrified as far as Rickmansworth. Today, the only significant change is that Jubilee Line services replaced those of the Bakerloo over the line to Stanmore from 1 May 1979.

26 November 1965 (A155724)

Hampton Court

With Hampton Court Palace located slightly to the north over the River Thames, the attractive terminus at Hampton Court echoes the Jacobean-style building being designed by Sir William Tite and built in red brick. The 1.75-mile long branch from Hampton Court Junction, just to the west of Surbiton, was opened by the LSWR on 1 February 1849. Although the then chairman of the LSWR, W. J. Chaplin, was unenthusiastic about the construction of the line, the branch proved to be a considerable success. Passenger services over the Hampton Court branch were electrified from 18 June 1916. The small goods yards, with a shed also in a mock Jacobean style, can be seen alongside the passenger terminus in this 1955 photograph. Freight facilities were withdrawn from Hampton Court on 3 May 1965. If only traffic across the River Thames at Hampton Court was as light 50 years on!

4 October 1955 (F25861)

Harrow & Wealdstone

Located on the West Coast main line, Harrow & Wealdstone was the junction for the ex-LNWR branch line that served Stanmore. This view, looking in the down direction, shows to good effect the facilities on offer at the station just before the outbreak of World War 2. The two westernmost platforms (on the LNWR 'New Line' opened in 1912) saw electric services introduced to Watford on 16 April 1917. A three-car rake of Oerlikon stock can be seen in the down platform. Beyond the station, on the north side, several rakes of Bakerloo Line stock can be seen stabled. Bakerloo line services were extended north of Willesden Junction to Watford contemporaneously with the inauguration of LNWR electrified services in 1917. Harrow & Wealdstone is now the terminus of Bakerloo Line services, although these ceased north of Stonebridge Park for a brief period in the early 1980s. The easternmost platform was used for the branch line to Stanmore; this line was opened under the auspices of the Harrow & Stanmore Railway on 18 December 1890. Passenger services over the branch were withdrawn on 15 September 1952 and the final section of the line, freight to Belmont, ceased on 5 October 1964.

June 1937 (53686)

Harrow & Wealdstone

Harrow & Wealdstone's place in railway history is ensured as a result of the railway accident that occurred here at 8.19am on 8 October 1952 when the 8.15pm Perth-Euston sleeper, hauled by No 46242 *City of Glasgow*, overshot signals and collided with the 7.31am local service from Tring hauled by 2-6-4T No 42389. A third train, the 8am express from Euston to Liverpool and Manchester hauled by No 45637 *Windward Islands* (acting as pilot) and No 46202, ploughed into the debris. A total of 112 people were killed with countless more injured. This photograph, taken later on the day of the accident, shows well the devastation wrought. The official report, compiled by Lt-Col G. R. S. Wilson, the then Chief Inspecting Officer of Railways in the Ministry of Transport, determined that the causes of the accident were solely the result of the up sleeper over-running the signals and that, once the first collision had occurred, there was nothing that the signalman could do to prevent the third train hitting the debris of the earlier accident. Along with the 112 fatalities both Nos 45637 and 46202 were also casualties.

8 October 1952 (R17939)

Hatfield

Located on the East Coast main line to the south of Welwyn Garden City, Hatfield was the junction for the ex-GNR branch towards St Albans, which can be seen heading towards the west in this view, as well as the point at which branch line services to Dunstable and Hertford, which deviated from the ECML at Welwyn Garden City, terminated. The main line through Hatfield opened on 7 August 1850 with the St Albans branch being authorised in 1862 and opened on 16 October 1865. Services from Hertford via Welwyn reached Hatfield in 1869 and those from Dunstable seven years later following the GNR's take-over of both routes. As can be seen, the facilities at Hatfield were significant in the late 1920s and evidence of at least three steam locomotives is clear in the photographs. As elsewhere, however, the post-World War 2 years have brought significant changes. The branch to St Albans closed to passenger services on 1 October 1951 and to freight on 5 October 1964; the trackbed of the line is now a cycleway. Both the Dunstable and Hertford lines are also now closed completely, although this did not directly influence the view pictured here. The station itself was rebuilt in the early 1970s and a further change came with the electrification of suburban services out of King's Cross when the ECML through Hatfield was energised at 25kV later in the same decade.

5 November 1928 (25382)

Haydons Lane

Viewed looking towards the east, with Wimbledon FC's Plough Lane ground and the Wimbledon Stadium in the background, this view records the station at Haydons Road on the Wimbledon-Tooting line. The Tooting, Merton & Wimbledon Railway was authorised in 1864 to construct a line from Streatham to Wimbledon via Tooting with a second route heading from Tooting via Merton to approach Wimbledon from the west. The line was jointly taken over by the LSWR and LBSCR in 1865 and was opened throughout on 1 October 1868. Services through Haydons Lane were electrified as from 3 March 1929. Today, the majority of services through Haydons Lane are operated by the First Capital Connect franchise with a number also operated by Southern.

5 May 1961 (A87219)

Hither Green

Located on the South Eastern Railway main line between Charing Cross and Tonbridge, the station at Hither Green opened on 1 June 1895, some 30 years after the route itself. The line through to Chislehurst opened on 1 July 1865 and the site became a junction the following year with the opening of the Dartford Loop, authorised on 30 June 1862, on 1 September 1866. The location's importance grew with the opening of the freight yards in 1899 at which time the Lee spur, from south to east, was also opened. As a freight centre, Hither Green's importance grew with the transfer from Southwark of the Continental freight depot on 10 October 1960. Clearly visible in this view taken looking towards the northwest are the ranks of housing constructed by speculative builders in the early 20th century; purchasers of the houses were encouraged to move to the area by the offer of free season tickets from the newly-opened station. Also visible, on the extreme left of the photograph, is the engine shed at Hither Green. This was originally constructed by the Southern Railway and opened on 10 September 1933. The shed closed to steam in October 1961 and was used as one of the SR's main diesel depots thereafter.

24 September 1964 (A14901)

Hornsey

Recorded looking towards the northeast, Hornsey shed is visible to the east of Hornsey station, which can be seen on the extreme left of this view. Although Hornsey station opened in 1850, the structure pictured here was built in the early 20th century. For the GNR, Hornsey was an important freight destination as it compensated for the relative shortage of siding accommodation south of Finsbury Park. The extensive goods yard was opened in 1885 and the up and down yards at Ferme Park, to the south of the station, followed in 1888. Slightly to the south of the station in this view can be seen a turntable; this represents part of a small locomotive facility established at the north end of the down Ferme Park sidings in 1891. The facilities, apart from a turntable, also included a coal stage. It has been suggested that the turntable was removed in 1929 but this photograph would suggest that it survived at least into the following year although it had disappeared slightly later. On the upside, Hornsey shed was an eight-road structure initially opened in 1899. Provided with a 52ft turntable and coaling stage, the shed was to remain unchanged until reroofing by BR in 1955. The shed lost its steam allocation in July 1961 and was then used as a diesel depot for a decade. It was subsequently utilised as part of the EMU depot constructed to serve the suburban electric services out of King's Cross.

1930 (31490)

Hounslow West

The future Piccadilly Line through Hounslow was first authorised as the Hounslow & Metropolitan Railway on 26 August 1880 when powers were obtained to construct a line from a junction slightly north of Acton Town station through to Hounslow Barracks. The first section of line, constructed with double track, opened as far as Hounslow High Street (Town) on 1 May 1883 with the section through to Hounslow Barracks being opened as a single-track line from Lampton Junction, slightly to the north of the original terminus, on 21 July 1884. initially, the station at Hounslow Barracks — Hounslow West from 1 December 1925 — was provided with a single platform, signalbox, station house and booking hall — ample provision for the services then provided. By the late 19th century the Hounslow branch was very much a backwater but this was to change in the early years of the 20th. The American owners of the Metropolitan District Railway planned both to take over the H&MR and electrify both it and the MDR proper. The MDR obtained powers for both the take over and the electrification and electric services commenced over the route on 13 June 1905. Doubling of the single-line section followed, with the final 62 chains to Hounslow West being completed on 28 November 1926 (more than a decade after the bulk of the work). At the same time as the line was doubled, a new station was constructed with three platforms; the original station building was rebuilt to a design of Charles Holden — illustrated in this view looking towards the west — being opened on 5 July 1931. Initially electric services were provided by the District Railway but from 8 February 1932 Piccadilly Line services also reached Hounslow West, in order to reduce congestion on the District, and from 13 March 1933 services were provided exclusively by the Piccadilly. Hounslow West was to remain the terminus of the branch for a further 40 years until the opening of the Piccadilly Line extension to Hatton Cross on 19 July 1975; the construction of this extension resulted in the slight relocation of the platforms at Hounslow with those illustrated in this view closing on 11 July 1975 and the new ones coming into use three days later.

6 May 1931 (39296)

Ilford

Pictured looking towards the west, this view of Ilford station, on the ex-GER main line between Liverpool Street and Chelmsford, shows the location as it existed shortly after the Grouping. Ilford was one of the original Eastern Counties Railway stations that opened with the line on 20 June 1839 although the station illustrated here was the result of expansion in the late 19th century to cater for the growing population and also for the opening of the Fairlop Loop line, which headed to the north from a junction to the east of Ilford and which opened on 1 May 1903. The scene as illustrated here was to change dramatically after World War 2 when the long-planned electrification of the suburban services was completed. This work included the construction of a flyover to the west of the station and a new EMU depot to the east. Following trial runs, the new 1,500V dc EMUs entered passenger service on 26 September 1949.

28 August 1928 (24245)

Kensington High Street

Viewed looking towards the northeast, with Kensington Palace in the distance, the station at High Street Kensington — known originally as Kensington (High Street) until the end of the 19th century — can be seen in the foreground. The Metropolitan Railway line from Paddington to South Kensington was authorised, as part of a scheme to construct an Inner Circle, on 29 July 1864 and the line opened on 1 October 1868 from Praed Street Junction, near Paddington, through Kensington High Street, to Gloucester Road; a connection from there to the newly opened Metropolitan District line at South Kensington was opened on the following 24 December. Relations between the Metropolitan and District Railways were not always harmonious, however, and disputes occurred about the division of revenue. In order to improve its own position, the District constructed an unauthorised route parallel to the Metropolitan Railway from Gloucester Road to High Street Kensington — the Cromwell Curve — over which services ran between 1 October and 10 November 1884 although the dispute was not finally settled until 1903. District Railway services from Earl's Court had already started to terminate at High Street Kensington following the opening of the west-north link in 1871. The section between High Street Kensington and Earls Court was to see experimental electrification in 1900 and, in 1901, with the acquisition of the District Railway by the American financier Charles Tyson Yerkes in the following year the process of converting the railway to electric traction was set in hand. By 5 November 1905 the process of converting the Circle Line to electric traction was complete with only a handful of steam-hauled services remaining. Today, High Street Kensington serves both the Circle Line and the District Line shuttle from Olympia; the latter service terminating here.

20 September 1964 (A139921)

Kentish Town

The complex junctions to the east of Gospel Oak station (2) are demonstrated to good effect in this view of the location taken looking towards the south. The ex-NLR Hampstead Junction line, which opened on 2 January 1860, can be seen coming in from the west (2) and curving through the station towards Camden Road to the south (3). Coming in from the south (4) is a link between Kentish Town on the Midland main line — which can be seen in the background running towards St Pancras (8) and towards Cricklewood (9); the main line was to open for freight between Bedford and London St Pancras on 8 September 1867 and to passenger services to Moorgate on 13 July 1868. Passenger services into St Pancras commenced on 1 October 1868. This curve can be seen running to Highgate Road Junction (11) on the line from Gospel Oak towards Upper Holloway (5). At the junction there was Highgate Road High Level station; this was opened in 1868 and closed in 1915. By the date of this photograph little evidence of the station remained. At a lower level a second line (7) can be seen emerging from the northeast; this forms a junction with the line toward Upper Holloway slightly to the east of the scene viewed here. This line curves to the south, having passed through the site of Highgate Road Low Level station (which closed in 1918 after a life of only 18 years), before reaching a junction (1). At this point one line (6) headed south towards Engine Shed Junction at Kentish Town on the ex-MR main line with the second (12) heading towards Carlton Road Junction to allow access to the ex-MR main line towards Cricklewood. Of the lines illustrated here, there have been two casualties since the date of the photograph: the line from Kentish Town Junction to Highgate Road Junction (4 to 11) closed completely on 19 January 1964 and that between Highgate Road Low Level and Engine Shed Junction (6 to 10) was to succumb on 11 January 1981 when passenger services from Barking were diverted from Kentish Town to Gospel Oak.

26 May 1973 (A112804)

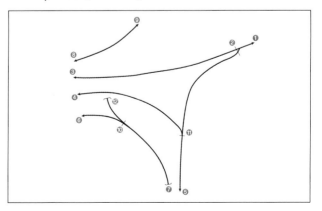

King's Cross

Viewed looking towards the west, this view shows to good effect the vast amount of land occupied by the railways immediately to the north of St Pancras and King's Cross stations. Dominating the centre of the view is King's Cross engine shed — known as 'Top Shed' — with the approach lines into St Pancras immediately to its west. On the right of the photograph, running from east to west, is the North London line with Camden Road station and junction visible in the distance. There was a station, called Maiden Lane, on the NLR route immediately to the north of King's Cross shed, but this closed in 1917 and by the date of this photograph all traces of this station would appear to be have been removed. Visible on the west side of the ex-MR approaches into St Pancras can be seen St Pancras goods; this was approaching the end of its career when recorded here as freight facilities were withdrawn from the yard in 1965. On the extreme left of the picture can be seen King's Cross goods; this opened in 1852 and was to survive until closure in 1973. The history of 'Top Shed' is fairly complex. The first phase of the development was the 25-road crescent shaped building located adjacent to the MR main line; this was opened originally in 1851 and was unique in that all tracks radiated from a single line rather than using a turntable. This structure was modified in 1862 when part was used as a carriage shed and the remainder for repairing locomotives. Simultaneously with this, a new eight-road shed was opened in front of the original shed. The next phase of the shed's life came in 1931 when the LNER modified the 1862 structure and recommissioned the part of the original building used as a carriage shed since 1862. The final development came in 1949 when both structures were reroofed by BR. In examining this photograph in detail it becomes clear that there is a dearth of locomotive stock on shed; the answer is straightforward — 'Top Shed' was formally closed three months earlier than the date of the photograph, on 17 June 1963, as part of the process by which East Coast main line services were dieselised. The new 'Deltics' were allocated to a new diesel depot at Finsbury Park and the old steam shed was surplus to requirements. It was subsequently demolished. At the time of writing this area of land is undergoing major redevelopment as part of the transfer of Eurostar services from Waterloo to the new international terminus at the enlarged St Pancras.

13 September 1963 (A119963)

Kingston

Viewed looking towards the east, Kingston station, with its two through platforms and bay platform at the west, is located on the loop line between Twickenham and New Malden. The station as illustrated here was the result of rebuilding in 1933/34. Originally the station comprised two elements: a street level terminus that opened with the line from Twickenham on 1 July 1863 and the through platform which opened with the line towards Surbiton on 1 January 1869. Also visible in the photograph is the extensive goods yard that once served the town; this closed in 1969. The goods shed, which was not finally demolished until 1995, was originally a two-road engine shed that opened with the line from Twickenham on 1 July 1863. The shed's facilities included a turntable and coal stage but was closed in 1907. Also visible in the foreground is the now closed line that served the gas works at Kingston. Apart from the railway interest, also identifiable in this view of Kingston is the old London Transport bus garage; a familiar site for enthusiasts for many years, this closed in 2000 and has since been redeveloped.

18 April 1962 (A99516)

Lewisham

A diesel-hauled freight passes through Lewisham station (1) towards Courthill Loop North Junction (3). In the foreground the ex-SECR line heads east towards Blackheath (2). From Loop North Junction, the line curves towards Courthill Loop South Junction (4) or heads under the main line towards Hither Green (5) to Ladywell Junction (7) on the line towards Catford Bridge (6). A spur links Ladywell Junction with the main line at Parks Bridge Junction (8). Out of the scene to the west, the main line and Blackheath routes meet at St Johns station (10) before heading in towards London Bridge (11). West of Lewisham station, a scissors junction allows trains also to head towards Nunhead (13) and there is also a connection, from Lewisham Vale Junction (9) to Tanners Hill Junction (12) from the Nunhead to London Bridge lines. Lewisham station originally dated to the opening of the line to Blackheath on 30 June 1849. It became a junction with the opening of the line towards Catford Bridge on 1 January 1857. The main line towards Hither Green opened in 1865 with the construction of the flyover (14) and loop being completed in 1929. This construction was designed to allow freight traffic to travel through Lewisham and gain access to the line to Nunhead (which had originally headed northeast towards Greenwich Park, Today the railway scene at Lewisham is more complicated, with the extension of the DLR south of Island Gardens now terminating in the 'V' formed by the station.

18 August 1970 (A207068)

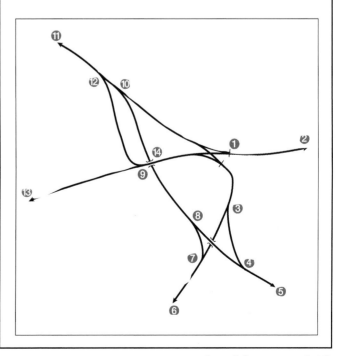

Limehouse

Viewed looking towards the north, the junction at Limehouse is pictured early in 1960. The first line to serve the area was the Commercial Railway, which had been incorporated on 28 July 1836 to construct a line between Minories and Blackwall; before the line opened the name had changed, courtesy of an authorised 415yd extension to Fenchurch Street, to the London & Blackwall Railway. The line, constructed to a gauge of 5ft 0in and cable hauled, opened on 6 July 1840 with a second track following on 3 August. The Fenchurch Street extension opened on 2 August the following year. The station here, originally called Stepney (it became Stepney East in 1923 and Limehouse in 1937) opened with the line in 1840. Initially, intermediate stations along the line were served by slip coaches. Stepney became a junction on 2 April 1849 with the opening of the line to Bow Junction; this was built to standard gauge and, in order to provide a connection, the L&BR was converted to standard gauge in 1848/49 and the cable haulage was replaced by steam. As a route into Fenchurch Street, the L&BR from Limehouse was used by North London services from 1850 and those of the London, Tilbury & Southend Railway from 1854. The third side of the triangle, from Salmons Lane Junction to Limehouse Junction, opened in 1880. Passenger services were withdrawn between Stepney East and Blackwall on 4 May 1926 and, by the date of this photograph, the original line from Limehouse towards Limehouse Junction had closed completely — on 14 April 1951 — although as can be seen the track at the western end was still extant in 1960 and used for the storage of wagons. Passenger services, electrified from 1949, continue to run from Fenchurch Street through Limehouse to Bow Junction; more recently the line eastwards has been reopened as part of the Docklands Light Railway.

April 1960 (A80064)

Liverpool Street/Broad Street

The proximity of these two termini is readily apparent in this view taken looking towards the east in 1957. The first of the two stations to be built, Broad Street, was the terminus of the North London Railway and opened to passenger traffic on 1 November 1865 and to freight on 18 May 1868. The NLR's goods yard was located to the north — ie here to the left — of the passenger station. The station was originally constructed with seven platforms, but was later extended to eight. Passenger services over the NLR were converted to electric operation on 1 October 1916. Freight facilities at Broad Street were withdrawn on 27 June 1969 and passenger services reduced to peak hours only in May 1985. Formal closure was approved in June 1985 and demolition started in November of the same year, as part of the massive Broadgate redevelopment, although final passenger services were not withdrawn until 30 June 1986. Beyond the redevelopment, the raised trackbed remains and the northernmost section through to Dalston is to see a revival courtesy of the expanded East London Line. Although the adjacent Liverpool Street station was also threatened with redevelopment, a campaign, led by the late poet laureate Sir John Betjeman, ensured that much of the trainshed was to survive. The first part of the ex-Great Eastern Railway station, serving suburban services, opened on 2 February 1874 with the remainder following on 1 November 1875, at which date the earlier station at Bishopsgate was closed. The station design was the work of Edward Wilson, the GER's engineer. His station saw trackwork modification in 1890 and an eastward extension four years later.

1 November 1957 (A69827)

London Bridge

It is only from the air that the scale of a station like that at London Bridge can be fully appreciated. First opened in mid-December 1836 by the London & Greenwich Railway, it is London Bridge that can claim to be the first of all London's terminal stations. The L&GR was joined in serving the station by the London & Croydon (later part of the London, Brighton & South Coast Railway) and the South Eastern Railway (which later built its own terminus at Bricklayers Arms (see p34). In order to accommodate the increased usage, the station was expanded in 1842 and again in 1864 when the through lines to Charing Cross were opened. London Bridge was a joint — in name but not in actions — station controlled by the SER and LBSCR, although competition meant that there was a wall — not breached until the creation of the SR in 1923 — between the two companies' sections. The approaches to London Bridge were widened twice — in 1866 and 1880 — to cater for the growth of traffic. Also constructed at the station was a hotel, although by the date of the photograph, this had already been converted to offices and largely destroyed during the war.

7 June 1955 (A59309)

Loughton

Viewed looking towards the southwest, a Central Line train approaches the station with a service for Epping. Although there had been earlier proposals, the first railway to reach Loughton was the Eastern Counties, which opened its seven-mile line to the town on 22 August 1856. The original station was located to the west of the station illustrated here and was used as a freight yard once the new station was completed. The station was relocated and converted into a through one with the opening of the 11.5-mile extension to Ongar on 24 April 1865. The line passed via the Great Eastern Railway to the LNER; however, in the 1930s, there were the first proposals for the transfer of the route to London Transport as part of a scheme to extend the Central Line. These plans were delayed by World War 2, but work started once peace was restored. Electric services were progressively extended along the line, with Loughton being reached on 21 November 1948. This was the terminus of electric services for less than a year before they were further extended to Epping on 25 September 1949. The station at Loughton was rebuilt as part of the electrification programme and freight facilities were withdrawn on 18 April 1966.

25 July 1963 (A118838)

Luton

Viewed looking northwards, this photograph shows the north end of Luton station. Dominating the scene is the ex-Midland Railway goods shed; notice running behind it one of the small open-top tramcars operated by Luton Corporation. By 1931, the electric trams were coming to the end of their life in the Bedfordshire town, the last operating in service on 16 April 1932. The ex-MR main line runs from west to east through Luton, whilst in the foreground can be seen the ex-Great Northern Railway route heading west from Luton (Bute Street) towards Dunstable, with the goods shed prominent in the foreground. Although Luton came to rely upon the ex-MR route, it was the future GNR line that was the first to serve the town. Opened on 3 May 1858, the line to Dunstable provided a link to the LNWR main line at Leighton Buzzard and it was the LNWR that operated the line until 1 September 1860 when the GNR opened its line eastwards towards Welwyn. The MR main line was to open for freight between Bedford and London St Pancras on 8 September 1867 and to passenger services to Moorgate on 13 July 1868. Passenger services into St Pancras commenced on 1 October 1868.
The scene records the ex-MR station in the years just prior to its rebuilding in 1937-1940. Also visible in the photograph is evidence of the locomotive servicing facilities provided by both the MR and GNR. The small turntable located at the west end of the station represented the MR's facilities whilst west of the GNR goods shed on the northern side of the line is the site of the GNR shed. The GNR shed closed about 1901 when most of the structure was demolished; the remains of the building were used as a store until October 1970 when it was completely demolished. Passenger services were withdrawn between Dunstable and Hatfield on 26 April 1965 (the section between Dunstable and Leighton Buzzard had ceased on 2 July 1962). In 1966 a connection was installed to the south of the two stations allowing freight services to access the Dunstable line from the ex-MR route, thus allowing the ex-GNR line east from Luton to close completely on 3 January 1966. Currently the Dunstable line is mothballed (since 30 April 1989) and the connection has been severed.

May 1931 (35122)

Marylebone

Although Marylebone was the last of the great London termini to be constructed, as can be seen the scale of the Great Central's facilities at its London terminus were impressive. The GCR's London Extension was opened to freight on 27 July 1898 and to passenger services on the following 15 March. This view, taken looking northwestwards shows the approaches to the station from the north. In the distance is the home of cricket, Lords Cricket Ground, and the railway can be seen emerging from Lord's Tunnel under Wellington Road. To the east of the Great Central lines are those of the Metropolitan Railway, which quickly disappear into tunnel again as they head towards Baker Street. The scale of the Great Central's goods yard and shed is apparent on the down side, whilst on the upside can be seen the carriage sheds; these were later to be converted for use as the depot servicing the DMUs used on the suburban services. Although Marylebone itself did not have an immediately adjacent locomotive shed, limited facilities were provided, including a turntable; the photograph postdates the construction in the 1930s by the LNER of a mechanical coaler. In the foreground of the photograph can be seen the trainshed of Marylebone station and, beyond it, part of the Great Central hotel. Designed by Sir R. W. Edis, this was opened in 1899 but was destined to have a relatively short life as a hotel under railway ownership, being converted to offices in 1945. The building served as the headquarters of British Rail from 1948 until its sale in 1986. Although services into Marylebone were once threatened and, indeed the facilities were much reduced, such has been the success of the line in recent years that additional platform capacity has been installed to replace that lost during rationalisation.

9 May 1946 (A548)

Marylebone Goods

With the familiar sight of Lords cricket ground in the foreground, the ex-Great Central main line can be seen emerging from Lord's Tunnel on its final approaches to Marylebone station. The station itself can be seen in the top right corner of the photograph beyond the Rossmore Road road bridge. To the north of the road bridge, on the down side, can be seen the enormous goods warehouse built for the GCR and, further to the north, the curved shed adjacent to the canal wharf. On the upside, beyond the carriage sidings and shed north of the road bridge, which were later converted to accommodate the DMUs that replaced steam on suburban services out of Marylebone, can be seen a turntable; this was part of a small locomotive servicing facility at Marylebone. This opened with the opening of the line and was to receive a mechanical coaler in 1937. The facility was closed by BR in 1966. Alongside the turntable and running parallel to the GC main line is the Metropolitan Railway route north from Baker Street; this was the first railway in this area and opened in 1868. At the point at which the Metropolitan Railway passed into Lord's Tunnel was Lord's station; known earlier as St John's Wood and St John's Wood Road, this station had opened with the railway in 1868 but was to be closed on 20 November 1939 and never reopened. The GCR's London Extension was opened to freight on 27 July 1898 and to passenger services on the following 15 March. Freight facilities were removed from the goods yard on 28 march 1966.

1923 (9093)

Merton Abbey

There are relatively few suburban lines in south London that have been closed completely but the line from Merton Park to Tooting is one of them. There was one intermediate station on the line — Merton Abbey — and this view records this station looking towards the north. The Tooting, Merton & Wimbledon Railway was authorised in 1864 to construct a line from Streatham to Wimbledon via Tooting with a second route heading from Tooting via Merton to approach Wimbledon from the west. The line was taken over jointly by the LSWR and LBSCR in 1865 and was opened throughout on 1 October 1868. By the date of the photograph, 21 June 1929, passenger services over the Merton Park-Tooting section had already been withdrawn, these ceasing on 3 March 1929 with the electrification of the lines through Tooting and Merton Park to Streatham and towards Sutton respectively. The line was, however, to remain open for freight to Merton Abbey. The section eastwards to Tooting was to close completely on 5 August 1968 but the final section, from Merton Abbey to Merton Park was not to close finally until 5 May 1975.

21 June 1929 (C18496)

Mill Hill

Taken shortly after the London, Midland & Scottish Railway had been created, this view of Mill Hill shows the ex-Midland Railway station with the four-track main line heading northwards. Out of view to the south is the ex-Great Northern Railway (by 1924 LNER) route to Edgware. The GNR line towards Edgware opened on 22 August 1867. This meant that the GNR reached Mill Hill slightly earlier than the MR, whose route southwards from Bedford to St Pancras opened for freight on 8 September 1867 and for passenger services to Moorgate on 13 July 1868. Passenger services started to serve St Pancras on 1 October 1868. The photograph illustrates well the traditional Midland Railway station with the platform canopies. The ex-MR station acquired the suffix 'Broadway' in 1950. Although Mill Hill Broadway continues to provide passenger facilities today for suburban services over the ex-Midland main line, the scene today is radically different, largely as a result of the construction of the M1 and the growth of housing in the area. Freight facilities were withdrawn from the small yard in August 1964.

1924 (10719)

Morden

Viewed looking towards the south, this view shows in the foreground the southern terminus of the Northern Line with, beyond the road bridge, the extensive 33-road Northern Line depot at Morden. Known as the Northern Line from 1937, the Charing Cross, Euston & Hampstead Railway was extended from the Strand (now Charing Cross) station to Charing Cross (now Embankment) station on 6 April 1914. It was to be extended south to Kennington, where it joined the City & South London Railway route to Clapham Common on 13 September 1926. On the same day the five-mile extension to Morden was also opened. Initially, there were plans for the further extension of the Underground line to the southwest in order to exploit the growing residential population between Wimbledon and Sutton; in the event, however, agreement was reached with the Southern Railway and the latter built its route between the two towns.

4 July 1964 (A132900)

Muswell Hill (Cranley Gardens)

The branch from Highgate to Muswell Hill and
Alexandra Palace, promoted by the Muswell Hill
Railway, was authorised on 13 May 1864 and opened on
24 May 1873 contemporaneously with the Palace itself.
All went well for a brief period but, on 9 June 1873,
the Palace was consumed by fire — the first of several
occasions when this popular attraction was to be so
destroyed and services over the branch were suspended.
The line was to reopen, again with the Palace, on 9 June
1875, but such was the line's precarious existence that it
was to close and reopen no fewer than seven times
between 1875 and 1898. Cranley Gardens station
opened on 2 August 1902. It was only in 1911 that
ownership of the line passed to the Great Northern
Railway, viewed looking to the north, the two-platform
station with its goods yard is visible in the centre.
Shortly after the date of this photograph, in 1932, plans
were drawn up for the transfer of the ex-GNR lines in
the area to be transferred to the London Passenger
Transport Board and electrified as part of an expanded
Northern Line. Although some work was completed by
1941, World War 2 intervened and by the cessation of
hostilities in 1945 costs had spiralled and, in February
1954, the remaining part of the project was abandoned.
Passenger services were withdrawn over the line on 5 July
1954, after which date the line to Alexandra Palace
closed completely; freight was withdrawn from Cranley
Gardens on 18 May 1957 and the branch closed
completely. The section from Cranley Gardens to
Muswell Hill (see p2) closed on 14 June 1956.

3 June 1932 (38225)

New Beckenham

Viewed looking towards the northeast, an eight-car EMU heads into New Beckenham station in the up direction. In the foreground can be seen New Beckenham Junction, with the line towards Beckenham Junction heading towards the east whilst the line towards Elmers End and Hayes heads off to the south. The first route to reach New Beckenham Junction was the Mid-Kent Railway — later South Eastern Railway — line from Lewisham which opened on 1 January 1857 and which terminated at Beckenham. New Beckenham became a junction with the opening of the line to Addiscombe on 1 April 1864. The original station at New Beckenham, opened contemporaneously with the line to Addiscombe, was sited slightly to the south of the junction and was relocated to the position recorded here in 1866. Electric services were introduced to Addiscombe on 28 February 1926.

30 June 1951 (R14880)

New Southgate

Viewed looking towards the north, New Southgate station with its four platforms can be seen astride the East Coast Main Line. Built by the Great Northern Railway, the East Coast main line, from the company's original terminus at Maiden Lane, opened on 7 August 1850. The original station here, called Colney Hatch & Southgate, located on the 1 in 200 gradient between Wood Green and Barnet, opened in 1850; the station illustrated in this view dates from reconstruction in 1890. As can be seen, the station is provided with two island platforms linked by a footbridge to the booking hall.

27 March 1968 (A178929)

Nine Elms

With the ex-LSWR main line stretching eastwards through Vauxhall to Waterloo, the area between the railway and River Thames is dominated by part of the complex network of sidings and sheds that once formed the goods yard at Nine Elms. Nine Elms had been the original terminus of the London & Southampton Railway when the line opened on 21 May 1838. Located at the edge of the then built-up area, the station was convenient for the river steamers but poorly located for those requiring quick access to the City. On 31 July 1845 the railway obtained powers to build a two mile extension from Nine Elms to Waterloo Bridge; the new route was built on a viaduct and opened on 11 July 1848. The viaduct was widened to provide eight running lines during the early years of the 20th century. Freight facilities were withdrawn from Nine Elms in 1968 and transferred to South Lambeth and the site subsequently redeveloped.

5 May 1938 (57041)

Nine Elms

Viewed looking towards the south, in the foreground can be see the major engine shed constructed by the LSWR at Nine Elms and, to the shed's east, the buildings that once formed Nine Elms Works. The first engine shed constructed at Nine Elms was opened with the London & Southampton Railway on 21 May 1838; this was replaced by a second shed in 1865, which lasted until 1876. The third phase was the construction of a semi-roundhouse shed located between the shed as illustrated here and the works; this had been built in 1876 and demolished in 1909. The next phase, and the first part of the shed still extant in this view, was the 'Old Shed' which was built in 1885 and provided with 15 roads; this is the part on the extreme right of the photograph although as illustrated here it had been damaged during World War 2 and repaired. Adjacent to the 'Old Shed', the 'New Shed' was built in 1910; this was a 10-road shed. The whole of the Nine Elms shed closed with the end of SR steam on 9 July 1967 and the site was subsequently cleared and redeveloped with part being used for the relocated Covent Garden Market.

20 June 1960 (A81078)

Norwood

Pictured shortly after it closed, the concrete-built shed at Norwood Junction can be seen at the centre of this view taken looking towards the west in late 1964. Although there had been an earlier shed at Norwood, this particular shed had been built by the Southern Railway and opened in 1935. The facilities provided included a 65ft turntable, coaling stage and water tower. Coded 75C in 1959, the shed's allocation in that year comprised six 'Q' class 0-6-0s, 'W' class 2-6-4Ts, two 'E3' 0-6-2Ts, one 'E6' 0-6-2T and 10 'C2' 0-6-0s. The shed closed to steam on 6 January 1964 and was later demolished. In this view the line towards Crystal Palace can be seen heading towards the northwest (1) and that north towards Sydenham (2). To the east the line heads towards Beckenham Junction (3) and to the south towards Norwood Junction station (4). Spurs link the line from Norwood Junction towards the Crystal Palace line via Bromley Down Junction (5) and Bromley Up Junction (6). Finally, there is also a spur between the Beckenham line at Spur Junction (7) southwards towards Norwood Junction itself. The first railway to serve Norwood — although the station was first called Jolly Sailor when it opened — was the London & Croydon, which opened on 5 June 1839; the present Norwood Junction station is situated slightly to the south of the original station and opened on 1 June 1859. The line from Crystal Palace to Norwood opened in 1857 and the section to Beckenham Junction on 3 May 1858. The spur from Norwood Junction towards Beckenham opened in 1862; this line lost its regular traffic on 11 September 1959 but was not to close completely until 1966. It was dismantled in 1972.

7 September 1964 (A138916)

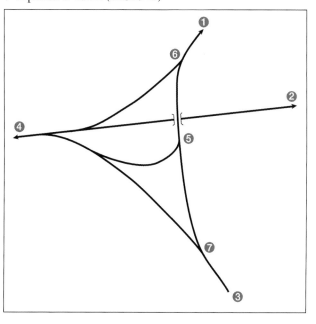

Paddington

The sheer acreage occupied by the passenger and freight facilities at Paddington is made explicit in this view taken looking towards the east with the Paddington canal basin in the background. In the foreground, on the north side of the passenger lines, is the Bishop's Road goods shed described on the next page. This view, however, is dominated by the scale of the terminus of the Great Western Railway and of the station hotel at its eastern end. Constructed between 1850 and 1854, the original station was the work of Isambard Kingdom Brunel and Matthew Digby Wyatt. As originally built, the station comprised three trainsheds: the central one being 102ft wide with the side sheds being 70ft and 68ft in width and a total length of 700ft. The station was originally provided with 10 platforms: three arrival, two departure and five for carriage storage. The departure side of the new station opened on 16 January 1854 and the arrival platforms on 29 May 1854. At that date the original GWR station, on the Bishop's Road site, was to close. The station cost a total of £650,000. The fourth trainshed, visible in this view on the north side, was added between 1909 and 1916 and is 109ft in width. The station hotel, designed by Philip Charles Hardwick, was not part of the original Brunel scheme but was opened slightly later than the station on 9 June 1854.

2 June 1947 (A6462/47)

Paddington

Viewed looking towards the west, the vast scale of the GWR's goods depot is all too apparent in this view taken in 1958. The first depot to be constructed on this site was built in 1858. New offices were opened in March 1906 on Bishop's Road for the purposes of centralising the administration of goods traffic. These are shown in this photograph on the left hand side of the photograph alongside the Bishop's Road. By the early years of the 20th decade, the existing goods depot was becoming increasingly inadequate to deal with the quantity of freight passing through; by the early 1920s a total of some 670 wagon movements a day were being handled on average, plus some 900 road wagons arriving and departing. Thus, in 1925, the GWR decided to rebuild and enlarge the existing depot. This work was completed by the early 1930s and enlarged depot is that illustrated in the photograph. Despite the vast amount of traffic that the depot once handled, it could not avoid the effects of the growth of the road haulage industry and, in August 1969, the first rationalisation occurred when a number of sidings were taken out of use. In 1970, the whole building was taken over by National Carriers although it remained rail-served until final closure came in December 1975. The depot then stood empty for a decade until demolition in March 1986.

19 September 1958 (A73565)

Poplar

A busy scene on East India Dock Road in 1935 sees no fewer than four trams and four buses passing the ornate entrance to the East India Docks. Three tram routes — Nos 65, 67 and 69 — passed along the road at this point; by this date all were operated by the London Passenger Transport Board but, prior to the creation of the LPTB in 1933, trams from the London County Council, East and West Ham corporations and Barking UDC would have passed this spot. By the date of the photograph, trams in east London were under severe threat with the LPTB having adopted a policy of tram to trolleybus conversion. At this point the trams were powered by current drawn from the conduit; it was only to the east of this point that conventional overhead was used. However, the arrival of the trolleybuses meant the installation of overhead along the East India Dock Road. The surviving two tram routes at this point were converted to trolleybus operation on 9 June 1940. The trams illustrated are probably ex-LCC 'E' class cars dating originally from 1905/6 although refurbished in 1927-30. In the foreground, apart from the entrance to the East India Docks themselves can be seen the then entrance to the Blackwall Tunnel. Also in the foreground can be seen part of the extensive lines that once served London's massive dockyard capacity. These lines, like the trams and the East India Docks themselves, are now all part of history.

1935 (46628)

Putney Bridge

Viewed looking southwards towards East Putney station in the distance, Putney Bridge station on the District Line can be seen in the foreground with Fulham Bridge crossing the river. The section of the District Railway to Putney Bridge was opened on 1 March 1880 and extended south of the river to Wimbledon, sharing LSWR metals from East Putney, on 3 June 1889. Electrified services over the section to Putney Bridge commenced on 23 July 1905 and, following work by the LSWR, extended to Wimbledon on 27 August the same year.

12 May 1958 (A70745)

Queens Park

Viewed looking west, Queens Park station, serving the Bakerloo and suburban lines into London Euston can be seen towards the top right of the photograph beyond the Salisbury Road bridge. The London & Birmingham Railway — later the London & North Western — opened from Euston Square to Boxmoor on 20 July 1837 but it was not until 1879 that Queens Park station opened. The Bakerloo line, which emerges to the surface just to the south of the station, between the main line and the Bakerloo's two-track South Shed, opened from Kilburn Park to Queens Park on 11 February 1915 and was extended thence to Willesden on 10 May 1915. Visible to the north of the station is the four-track North Shed. Freight facilities, visible in the foreground, were withdrawn from Queens Park on 6 July 1964.

28 August 1963 (A119667)

Richmond

Pictured in the late 1920s looking towards the northeast, this fascinating view of Richmond shows to good effect the two stations that existed at Richmond before the rebuilding of the late 1930s that saw the construction of a single station. Running from east to west is the LSWR line from Barnes to Staines; this was opened to Richmond on 17 July 1846 and extended to Datchet on 22 August 1848. The original terminus, used from 1846 until 1848, was on the site of the goods yard on the south side of the station illustrated here. Richmond's third station, the four-platform terminus known as Richmond New, opened on 1 January 1869. This was used for North London Railway services but its importance increased with the construction of connections to the Hammersmith & City (at Grove Junction) and to the District (at Studland Road Junction) on 1 June 1877. These connections allowed the H&C and District, as well as the GWR, to serve Richmond, although both the GWR and H&C ceased to operate to the town on 31 December 1910 and in 1906 respectively. The District Railway services were electrified from 1 August 1915 and those of the NLR on 1 October 1916. Electric services over the LSWR line started on 30 January 1916. Richmond station was rebuilt in the mid-1930s, with the now unified structure being opened on 1 August 1937. Freight facilities were withdrawn from the town on 6 May 1968.

15 August 1928 (22843)

Shepherds Bush

With two of London's most familiar buildings — the BBC Television Centre and the White City Stadium — dominating this view looking towards the north shows, in the foreground, White City station on the Metropolitan (now Hammersmith & City) Line to Hammersmith. This station was known as Wood Lane from its opening in 1908 until 1959. Passing under the Metropolitan Line is the Central Line with White City station (opened in 1947) prominent. Heading north from White City, the line curves to the west and a link, from Wood Lane Junction to Viaduct Junction, can be identified heading to the east. This provided a connection to the West London line, which can be seen running from north to south in the of right hand corner of the photograph. The first line to serve the area was the West London line, which opened from Willesden Junction to Kensington on 27 May 1844. The Metropolitan line, from Westbourne Park, was constructed as a broad gauge route and opened by the GWR on 13 June 1864. The line became jointly owned with the Metropolitan on 15 July 1867 with the Metropolitan operating passenger services. The line was converted to standard gauge in August 1868 and electrified from 5 November 1906. The Central Line opened to a station called Wood Lane, located slightly to the south of White City station, on 14 May 1908; this station closed with the opening of the new White City station. The line from the Ealing direction, promoted as the Ealing & Shepherd's Bush Railway, was opened for freight to Viaduct Junction on 16 April 1917 with the tube connection with Wood Lane opening on 3 August 1920. The section west of Wood Lane Junction was quadrupled in 1938, although this was reduced to two tracks after 9 March 1964 when the link between Viaduct Junction and Wood Lane Junction closed completely. Another notable casualty in this view is the White City stadium itself; built for the 1908 Olympics and reused for the games 40 years later, the stadium closed in 1984 and was subsequently demolished to allow for expansion of the BBC facilities at the site.

9 September 1961 (A95444)

Shepperton

Promoted by the Thames Valley Railway, incorporated in 1862, the 6.5-mile long branch from Strawberry Hill to Shepperton was opened on 1 November 1864. Originally, the line had been conceived to extend westwards towards Chertsey, with the result that Shepperton station was designed as a through station, situated at some distance from the actual village of Shepperton (which is situated on the banks of the River Thames. The extension was, however, never constructed, leaving the station to serve as a terminus. The main station building was situated on the notional down platform, with a small shelter on the up. Also provided was a signalbox, turntable, water tower and goods shed, all clearly visible in the aerial view taken in the late 1920s. The Shepperton branch was electrified on 30 January 1916 and an EMU can be seen in the station. The relative under-development of the scene at this time is instructive as, inevitably, the area around the railway was heavily developed from the 1930s onwards. One notable development was the construction of Terminal House, home for many years of Ian Allan Publishing, at the western end of the site in 1962. Freight facilities were withdrawn from Shepperton on 1 August 1960. The original station building was demolished in the mid-1980s and replaced by a new structure, Clock House, which again was home for a period of Ian Allan Publishing.

10 September 1928 (23495)

Southall

Viewed from the west, this view shows the station at Southall on the ex-GWR main line out Paddington shortly after the Nationalisation of the railways. At this date the station possessed six platforms. The southernmost platform served the Brentford branch; this broad-gauge branch opened to freight traffic on 18 July 1859 and to passenger services on 1 May 1860. However, by the date of the photograph, passenger services had already been withdrawn — on 4 May 1942 — although the line remained open — as it does in 2006 — for freight traffic. The next two platforms were on the fast lines, the next two were the relief lines used by local services, and the northernmost platform, as evinced here, was largely used for parcels traffic. Alongside the stock in this platform can be seen an 0-6-2T. Out of view to the east of the station are the steam depot, the Brentford branch curving to the south, sidings to local factories and the famous AEC factory. Alongside the station, on the south side, three coaches including an auto-trailer can be seen stabled. Prominent in the photograph is the Batchelors Peas building; this was for a period the home of the Great Western Preservation Group.

6 July 1948 (A17060/48)

St Pancras

Viewed looking towards the southeast, this view shows
to good effect the dramatic trainshed roof at St Pancras
stations. In the right foreground can be seen part of the
large Somers Town goods depot (closed 1975) and to the
east of St Pancras station the curved lines of the Great
Northern Hotel and beyond that King's Cross station.
Visible in the foreground, at the country end of the
station, can be seen an '08' shunter and Class 25
diesel-electric. The trainshed, with its span of 243ft, was
designed by William Henry Barlow and R. M. Ordish
and was at the time of its construction the largest single-
span trainshed built in the world. The cast iron support
work for the roof was supplied by the Butterley Iron Co
in Derbyshire. The roof is tied together by floor girders
in the station floor, which is itself supported by a grid of
iron columns. The space thus created under the
platforms was used to store one of the most important
freight items brought to London by the MR — beer
from Burton on Trent. The 500-bedroom Midland
Grand Station hotel beyond, constructed to the design of
Sir George Gilbert Scott, was built between 1868 and
1876, although opened in May 1873, in a Gothic style
which was to prove highly influential in future railway
work. The construction of Liverpool Street station, from
1875 onwards, to the design of Edward Wilson also
adopted the increasingly fashionable Gothic style whilst
William Peachey of the North Eastern Railway also
echoed Scott's work when he redesigned stations at
Middlesbrough and Sunderland.

9 June 1964 (A130166)

St Pancras

Viewed towards the northeast the contrasting styles of the ex-Midland Railway at St Pancras, closest to the camera, and the ex-Great Northern terminus at King's Cross are readily apparent in this view taken in the early 1960s. On the extreme left of the photograph is the MR's Somers Town goods yard; this was, by this date entering the twilight of its career. Freight facilities were withdrawn on 5 June 1967 and it was to close completely on 23 April 1968 when coal traffic ceased; it is now the site of the British Library. Initially, MR services terminated at King's Cross, but the company opened an extension to its new terminus from Bedford for freight on 8 September 1867, to local traffic to Moorgate on 13 July 1868 and to St Pancras itself on 1 October 1868. The trainshed, with its 243ft span, was designed by W. H. Barlow and R. M. Ordish whilst the neo-Gothic Midland Great Hotel was designed by one of the most eminent of Victorian architects, Gilbert Scott. By the date of the photograph, the hotel had closed and had been converted into offices. Midland Main Line services continue to serve St Pancras, although the station is now undergoing major restoration in connection with its use for Eurostar services to Paris and Brussels from 2007. The first railway to reach this location was the GNR and King's Cross station was to open on 14 October 1852. The station was designed by Lewis Cubitt and featured two train sheds. These were originally constructed with laminated timber ribs, but these were later replaced by iron. The Great Northern Hotel followed in 1854. The station was provided with additional platforms in the 1860s and 1870s primarily to serve local trains. King's Cross remains the southern terminus for express services over the East Coast main line and for suburban services to Peterborough and Cambridge. The extensive freight facilities provided by the GNR can be seen towards the top left of the photograph; these have largely disappeared and the site incorporated into the massive redevelopment scheme linked to the Eurostar terminal.

8 October 1964 (A143772)

Stanmore

Although Stanmore was served by a branch off the West Coast main line from Harrow & Wealdstone, the area was still very rural when the branch of the Metropolitan Railway opened on 10 December 1932 — as is all too evident in this photograph showing the terminus some four years after the line opened. Although today the foreground is still largely undeveloped, the area to the east and west of the station has been built over with much of this development occurring before the outbreak of World War 2. This was the last extension to the Underground network completed before the creation of the London Passenger Transport Board under whose auspices services were switched from the Metropolitan Line to the Bakerloo line on 20 November 1939. In 1977 a further change saw Stanmore become the northern terminus of the new Jubilee Line.

16 June 1936 (R1574)

Stonebridge Park

A familiar sight to passengers heading into and out of London Euston, the true scale of the sidings between Willesden and Stonebridge Park only becomes apparent in an aerial view such this. Pictured looking towards the west, the now-electrified West Coast main line running from Euston (1) towards Wembley (2) can be clearly seen. On the north side the combined Watford/Bakerloo lines from Harlesden (4) can be seen curving under the WCML before heading towards Watford (3) having past through Stonebridge Park station (5). To the north of Stonebridge Park station can be seen the LUL Bakerloo Line depot and the main Heavy Repair Shop (6). To the south of the WCML can be seen Willesden 'F' Sidings; these are linked to the Low Level goods lines (11) which can be seen passing under the WCML towards the bottom of the photograph. At the western end of the yard can be seen Wembley InterCity depot (8); this is used for the storage and maintenance of rolling stock used on main line services out of Euston. In the foreground can be seen Willesden Brent Sidings (10) with Willesden Brent Sidings signalbox (9) located at the western end; this is an LNWR-built structure dating originally to 1878. Between Willesden Brent Sidings and Wembley depot can be seen Willesden 'D' (12) and 'E' (13) sidings. On the west of the WCML can be seen Nuttals sidings (7). The first railway to serve the area was the London & Birmingham, which opened north from Euston on 20 July 1837. Stonebridge Park station opened on 15 June 1912 with the completion of the New Lines, which opened on that date north of Willesden to Harrow. Bakerloo Line services reached Willesden on 10 May 1915 and were extended north to Watford Junction on 16 April 1917.

August 1967 (A177294)

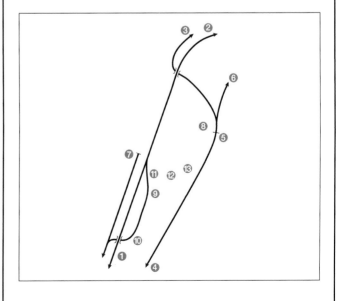

Stratford

The east London junction at Stratford has always been important and, with the arrival of the Docklands Light Railway (1987) and Jubilee Line (1999) in the years since this photograph was taken, this importance has increased. Moreover, with the construction of the second phase of the Channel Tunnel Rail Link and associated international station due for completion in 2007, Stratford's importance can only increase. This view, taken towards the north, shows well the extent of the railway at Stratford prior to these developments. Stratford station (1), with platforms on both upper and lower levels, can be seen astride the ex-GER main line from Chelmsford (2) to Liverpool Street (3). From the main line, two spurs can be seen linking the east-west route with the north-south line from Hackney (8) to Woolwich (9): Woolwich Junction Main Line (4) to Woolwich Junction with Loop (5) and from Sheet Factory Junction (6) to the main line (7). Alongside the route towards Cambridge (11) can be Stratford depot (12) whilst coming in from the west can be seen the ex-GER line from Victoria Park. By the date of the photograph, Stratford Works had been closed and the site redeveloped; the works were located to the east of the depot and Cambridge line. The first railway to serve Stratford was the Eastern Counties Railway (later part of the GER) which opened between Devonshire Road and Romford on 18 June 1839. The route from the north opened on 15 September 1840 and that to North Woolwich on 14 June 1847. The Central Line extension, linked into the conversion of the Ongar branch, opened through Stratford on 4 December 1946. Since the photograph was taken, Stratford depot has closed and the two curves from Sheet Factory Junction and Woolwich Junction with Loop have also been removed.

11 August 1972 (A240768)

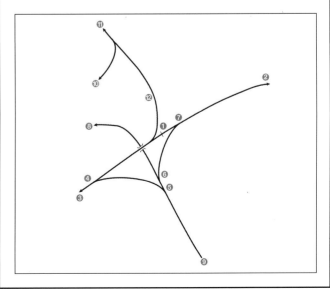

Streatham

Viewed towards the northwest, this view of Streatham sees Streatham Common station (1) in the foreground on the ex-LBSCR line from Balham (2) to Selhurst (3). From Streatham Common Junction (4) to Streatham Junction (5) there is a spur into the ex-LBSCR line from Tulse Hill (6) to Mitcham Junction (7). At Streatham South 'C' Junction (9) the ex-LSWR/LBSCR joint line to Wimbledon heads west (8) and from Streatham South 'B' (10) and Streatham South 'A' (11) junctions a link towards the Balham line at Streatham North Junction (12). Parallel to the Tulse Hill-Mitcham Junction line can be seen the Eardley carriage sidings (13). The first railway to serve the scene illustrated here was the line from Balham to Selhurst, which opened on 1 December 1862 and was quadrupled in 1903, with the route from Tulse Hill to Mitcham following, along with the spurs, on 1 October 1868. Today all the lines visible in the view are still operational although the Eardley carriage sidings have closed.

17 May 1963 (A111693)

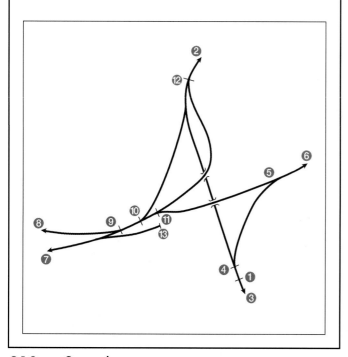

Surbiton

The original station, called Kingston, was located slightly to the north of the current station seen here looking in the up direction. This station opened with the London & Southampton line from Nine Elms on 21 May 1838. The station was moved to its present position in 1845 shortly before the opening of the line to Hampton Court, which leaves the main line slightly to the south of Surbiton at Hampton Court Junction. Kingston acquired its own station with the opening of the line between Twickenham and Raynes Park (in 1863 from Twickenham to Kingston and six years later from Kingston to Raynes Park). The station as seen in this post-World War 2 view was the result of rebuilding immediately prior to the war, being reconstructed as part of the electrification scheme for the main line from Surbiton through Woking to Guildford, Portsmouth and Farnham. Electric services over the newly converted lines started from Surbiton to Guildford and Farnham on 3 January 1937. They were extended from Guildford to Portsmouth on 29 May 1937 and from Farnham to Alton on 4 July. Surbiton was one of three stations reconstructed for the work, with the others being Havant and Woking. Visible in this view is the goods yard that served the town; freight facilities were to be withdrawn from Surbiton in 1971.

2 July 1949 (R11333)

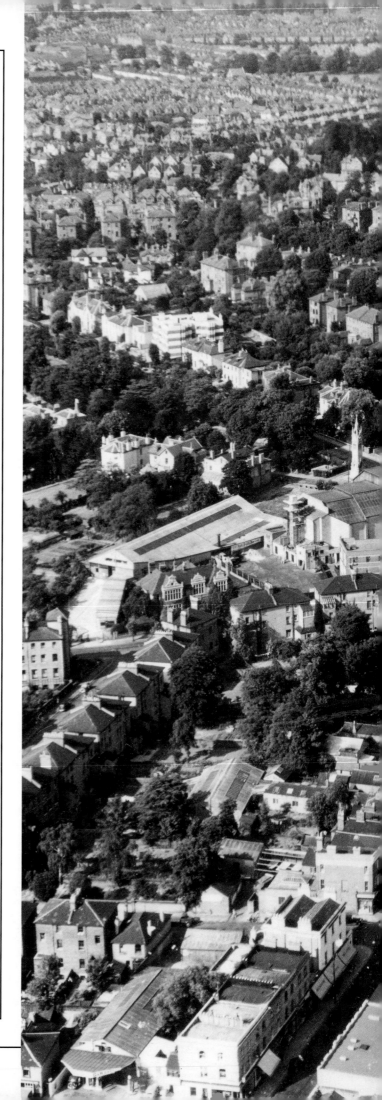

Sutton

One of the earliest views in this volume, this scene records the junction station at Sutton viewed looking towards the north. The original line to serve the town was the LBSCR route from West Croydon to Epsom; this opened on 10 May 1847. The station became a junction with the opening of the branch to Epsom Downs on 22 May 1865 and the line towards Peckham Rye on 1 October 1868. The Epsom Downs line is that which can be seen curving away from the station towards the southwest. The final phase in the railway development of Sutton came on 5 January 1930 with the completion of the line towards Wimbledon. On the down side of the Epsom Downs branch can be seen the goods yard; this was to close on 7 October 1968 and the site is now occupied by an office block.

25 June 1920 (1676)

Tattenham Corner

Promoted by the Chipstead Valley Railway, later part of the South Eastern Railway, the eight-mile branch from Purley to Tattenham Corner was opened from Purley to Kingswood on 2 November 1902 and thence to Tadworth on 1 July 1900. The final extension, to Tattenham Corner, opened on 4 June 1901. The branch was originally built as single track, but it was doubled when the extension to Tattenham Corner was opened. As one of the stations adjacent to the Epsom race course, Tattenham Corner is especially busy on race days most notably on Derby Day. It was to Tattenham Corner station that the Queen travelled by Royal Train when attending the race. Services over the Tattenham Corner branch were electrified from 25 March 1925 and in this 1970 view two- and four-car units can be seen in the station.

23 July 1970 (A206835)

Tilbury Riverside

Viewed looking towards the northeast, the impressive terminus at Tilbury Riverside, sited at the south of a triangular junction on the LT&SR, is seen in this view dating from the 1960s shortly after the electrification of the route. The LT&SR originally reached Tilbury from Forest Gate on 13 April 1854 with the line being extended eastwards later that year to Hordon (Stanford-le-Hope). Like the London & Blackwall and Eastern Counties railways, the LT&SR also acquired interests in ferry traffic and opened a second station serving Tilbury, Tilbury Docks, on 15 June 1885. Tilbury Riverside was constructed as a joint station and customs hall for the new landing stage, used by liners, that opened on 16 May 1930. In an era before air travel was generally accepted, there was significant traffic to be had in providing a link with the liners that called at Tilbury; in 1955, for example 500 liners called at the landing stage. However, as this traffic declined, so too did the importance of Riverside station. Electric services started operating at peak hours on the ex-LT&SR lines on 6 November 1961 with the full timetable commencing on 18 June 1962. Declining passenger traffic resulted in the closure of Tilbury Riverside station on 28 November 1993 although a freight depot now occupies part of the site, accessing the remaining ex-LT&SR line via the south to west curve.

18 September 1964 (A139939)

Tottenham

Viewed looking east and with the Lea Navigation running north-south, this photograph records, in the foreground, running from west to east, the Tottenham & Forest Gate Joint line from South Tottenham to Woodgrange Park; this line was originally owned by the London, Tilbury & Southend and Midland railways and thus passed to the exclusive control of the Midland when the MR took over the LT&SR on 1 January 1912. Heading from north to south is the Great Eastern Railway's Lea Valley line from Stratford through Lea Bridge towards Ponders End. Tottenham (Hale) station can be seen towards the left of the photograph.
This photograph was taken in 1923, shortly after the Grouping, when the MR line passed to the LMS and the GER route to the LNER. The extreme east of the view shows Lockwood Reservoir, whilst in the middle is a large camouflaged factory, reflecting the fact that World War 1 had recently ended and that, with the arrival of the Zeppelin, London had not been free of the consequences of war. Tottenham (Hale) was one of the original stations opened by the Northern & Eastern Co. This railway was incorporated on 4 July 1836 to construct a line from Cambridge to Islington. Financial exigencies forced the company to divert its approaches to London so that a junction could be made with the Eastern Counties at Stratford. The line from Stratford to Broxbourne, including the station at Tottenham, opened on 15 September 1840. The line was originally built to a gauge of 5ft, but this was converted to standard gauge in the autumn of 1844, by which time the N&E had been leased to the ECR. Both were ultimately to form part of the Great Eastern. The Tottenham & Forest Gate Railway — some six miles in length — was authorised in 1890, being jointly promoted by the LT&SR and the MR to provide a link between the lines of the two companies. It was opened throughout on 9 July 1894. Both lines remain operational today, although Tottenham Hale station was rebuilt in the late 1960s when it became an interchange station for the new Victoria Line.

1923 (6778)

Upminster

Photographed in 1934 towards the east, this view at Upminster shows the station and its environs immediately after the extension of the District line to the town and the construction of the sidings for the Underground stock to the east of the station. The first line to serve Upminster was the LT&SR cut-off route from Barking to Pitsea; this opened on 1 May 1885. Prior to the line's opening, two short branches from Upminster were sanctioned on 20 August 1883. These were to Grays, which opened on 1 July 1892, and to Romford, which opened on 7 June 1893. To the east of Barking, the LCC constructed between 1925 and 1933 the enormous Becontree estate and this placed additional strains on the existing transport resources. In order to accommodate District services to Upminster two additional running lines were provided to Upminster; these were opened on 12 September 1932. The District Line's sidings were extended in 1958 and a depot constructed. Also visible in the centre of this 1934 view is the small engine shed at the station; this was again of relatively recent construction, having been built in 1931 as a replacement to a shed opened in 1893. The earlier shed, located slightly to the east, had been demolished in connection with the construction of the District sidings. The new shed at Upminster was to survive until closure on 17 September 1956. Today, main line services — all electrified since 1962 with the exception of the Romford branch that was converted in 1986 — are operated by the contemporary successor to the LT&SR — c2c — and District Line services also still terminate at the station.

28 March 1934 (43923)

Uxbridge High Street

Although there were proposals as far back as 1861
to provide a link between the LNWR main line at
Rickmansworth and Uxbridge, it was not until the final
years of the 19th century that progress was made. On
2 August 1898 the GWR was authorised to construct
a short 1.75-mile from Denham to the town with the
intention that it would later be extended through to
Vine Street to provide a through route. Although limited
work was undertaken on this extension, the GWR
concluded that the investment required was much
greater than the likely returns merited. From the start the
branch was operated by steam railmotors from opening
on 1 May 1907 with freight commencing to a small yard
to the west of the station on 11 May 1914. Passenger
services were suspended, as a wartime economy, between
31 December 1916 and 1 May 1919 and, during 1917,
the line, which had been built as double track
throughout, was singled. After World War 1, passenger
services were normally hauled by 0-4-2Ts but all
passenger services were again withdrawn on 1 September
1939. All freight traffic was withdrawn, with the
exception of coal traffic, on 25 September 1939; the line
was to close completely when the coal traffic ceased on
2 April 1962. The photograph, taken in August 1920
shortly after the resumption of passenger services,
shows well the station building constructed on the
embankment ands its access via a footbridge and
walkway from the High Street.

August 1920 (1578)

Uxbridge Vine Street

One of two branches to join the GWR main line at West Drayton, the Uxbridge (Vine street) branch was actually the first GWR branch to be constructed in the London area. The Great Western & Uxbridge Railway obtained powers to construct the 2.5-mile long branch on 16 July 1846; however, this company was unable to raise the required funds and, on 22 July the following year, the GWR took over the powers. As construction had not yet taken place, the GWR was forced to seek an extension in 1853. The branch finally opened on 8 September 1856. Originally built as a broad gauge line, the branch was converted to standard gauge on 7/8 October 1871.

As built the station was provided with an overall wooden roof; this was, however, replaced in the 1930s with the canopy illustrated in the photograph. At the same time the original platform layout was replaced by the single island platform as shown. Until 1897 there had been a small engine shed at the station and a turntable was to last for a further two years before removal. At the time of the photograph, the branch was still operated by steam; this was replaced by DMU operation in September 1958 but, as from 27 July 1962, passenger services were reduced to peak hours only. Withdrawal of passenger services was foreshadowed by the Beeching Report and they were withdrawn on 8 September 1962. The line was singled on 18 October 1962 as a freight-only route and the signalbox was closed at the same time. Freight services continued to Vine Street until complete closure came on 24 February 1964.

15 May 1953 (41117)

Uxbridge

Although slightly damaged, this aerial view is of interest in that it portrays the original Metropolitan Railway terminus in Uxbridge on Belmont Road. Whilst the town was ultimately to possess two Great Western branches — serving High Street and Vine Street (see pp224-227) — it was the town's second railway that was to be the most important, providing as it did a direct connection with central London. The Harrow & Uxbridge Railway, incorporated on 6 August 1897, was promoted by the District Railway as an extension of its existing line, but the District's inability to raise the capital resulted in the line passing instead to the Metropolitan, with the District Railway having running powers. The line was opened on 4 July 1904 and was initially operated by steam. Electrification, clearly visible in the photograph by examining the track, was inaugurated on 1 January 1905, although District Railway services did not commence until 1 March 1910. The station was provided initially with a brick building on the down side and the shelter on the up platform, which was used by District and later Piccadilly trains, was added later. The station was closed on 4 December 1938 when services were relocated to a new station on the High Street and freight facilities were withdrawn from the yard shown in 1939.

5 March 1929 (25812)

Vauxhall

The original LSWR terminus serving London was at Nine Elms, but this was inconvenient in terms of proximity to the centre of London. As a result, the railway sought powers to construct a two-mile extension to a new station — the future Waterloo. The extension was authorised on 31 July 1845 and the new route, built on a sinuous viaduct to avoid Lambeth Palace, and station were opened on 11 July 1848. The only intermediate station was at Vauxhall. The station as illustrated in this 1955 view taken looking southwestwards is largely the product of rebuilding in the early years of the 20th century when Waterloo station was enlarged and the viaducts approaching the station widened to provide eight running lines. Fifty years on the station is largely unchanged although it now possesses an Underground connection, courtesy of the Victoria Line, and a bus interchange on the northern side. It is in the environs that the passengers see vast changes, with large new office blocks, including the headquarters of MI6, and flats surrounding it. Perhaps the most remarkable feature of this 1955 view is that, despite the frequency of services through the station, the Aerofilms photographer has managed to record the location completely devoid of passenger trains!

8 June 1955 (A59416)

Victoria

Viewed looking towards the northwest, this view shows
the approaches to Victoria station and the platform area
in the early 1960s before the modernisation of the late
1980s. The origins of the station and of the approaches
across the river date to the 1850s when the London,
Chatham & Dover and London, Brighton & South
Coast railways jointly promoted the Victoria Station &
Pimlico Railway, which was incorporated in 1858.
Although the relationship was never wholly harmonious,
the station grew to become one of the largest serving
London. The LBSCR platforms were opened on
1 October 1860; these were used by the LCDR from
3 December 1860 until its own platforms were opened
on 25 August 1862. As the GWR had running powers
into the station — indeed was a part owner of the
station until 1932 — some of the LCDR track was dual
gauge in order to accommodate the GWR's broad gauge
trains from Southall. The station was considerably
expanded prior to World War 1, the LBSCR section
being completed in 1908 and the SECR — as the
LCDR had become — in 1909. It was only with the
creation of the Southern Railway in 1923 that the
division of Victoria into two stations with separate
stationmasters ceased. It was in the year that this
photograph was taken, 1961, that Victoria became the
railway terminal for fast services to Gatwick Airport.
This traffic was the driving force behind the construction
of additional platform capacity in the 1980s and the
rafting over of the ex-LBSCR side of the station.

18 May 1961 (A88703)

Wandsworth

With both electric tramcars and motorbuses visible on the extreme left of the photograph travelling along St John's Hill, this photograph shows the approaches to Clapham Junction from the west a decade after the Grouping. The northernmost quartet of lines represent the ex-LSWR main line from Clapham Junction to Woking whilst furthest from the camera is the ex-LBSCR main line towards East Croydon and the South Coast. The route through Wandsworth was one of the earliest in the capital with the LSWR line originally opening on 21 May 1838 and the LBSCR, under the auspices of the West End & Crystal Palace Railway, on 29 March 1858. Both railway companies originally provided railway stations to serve the lines at this point: the LSWR station at Wandsworth was to close in 1863 with the opening of Clapham Junction and the LBSCR's New Wandsworth station was to survive for a further six years. More recently, it was in the cutting here that the 1988 Clapham accident occurred; the event is now marked by a monument above the cutting.

1934 (R1318)

Waterloo

The enormous trainshed of Waterloo station dominates the foreground in this view taken looking towards the north in 1960. The station originally dated to the extension of the LSWR from Nine Elms, which opened on 11 July 1848. The first station was extended in 1860 with the opening of the 'Windsor' line platforms at the northern end — these were to be replaced as part of the construction of the new international station that was opened to serve the Channel Tunnel in 1994 — and, in 1864, a link was constructed to the newly-opened SER line from Charing Cross — seen here in the distance across the river — to London Bridge. Waterloo Junction station — renamed Waterloo East on 2 May 1977 — was opened on the SER route on 1 January 1869. The link between the two stations was closed on 26 March 1911 as part of the process of rebuilding the main Waterloo station from 1909 onwards. The station as illustrated here is very much the product of this rebuilding programme and was, with the LSWR War Memorial and Victory Arch, officially opened on 21 March 1922. The track layout was modified during the mid-1930s. At the date of the photograph, although suburban services were now electrified as were main line services to Portsmouth, there was still steam on main line services to the West Country and Bournemouth, and evidence of the old order is apparent in the presence of a rebuilt Bulleid Pacific and an 'M7' 0-4-4T.

30 April 1960 (A80041)

Welwyn Garden City

One of a number of garden cities developed in the early 20th century. Although there was a small settlement before the development of the new town, it was in 1920 that the town's major development started under the auspices of a private company. This view, taken looking towards the west, shows the station opened by the LNER on 20 September 1926 to serve the growing population. The ex-GNR route through Welwyn opened in 1850 and, considerably to the north of the station, two branch lines diverged. These were the routes towards Hertford — opened on 1 March 1858 — and that to Luton — opened on 1 September 1860. Once these lines were absorbed by the GNR, they were extended southwards closer to Welwyn. At the date of this photograph traffic over both branches was still extant. However, passenger services over the Hertford line ceased on 18 June 1951 with the line closing completely on 23 May 1966; passenger services to Luton ceased on 26 April 1965 with freight being withdrawn on 3 January 1966. Shortly before the date of this photograph, on 15 June 1935, a serious accident occurred at Welwyn when 13 people were killed as a result of a collision. The confusion of the signalman, which contributed to the accident, led to a modification to signalling known as the 'Welwyn Block'.

30 July 1937 (54513)

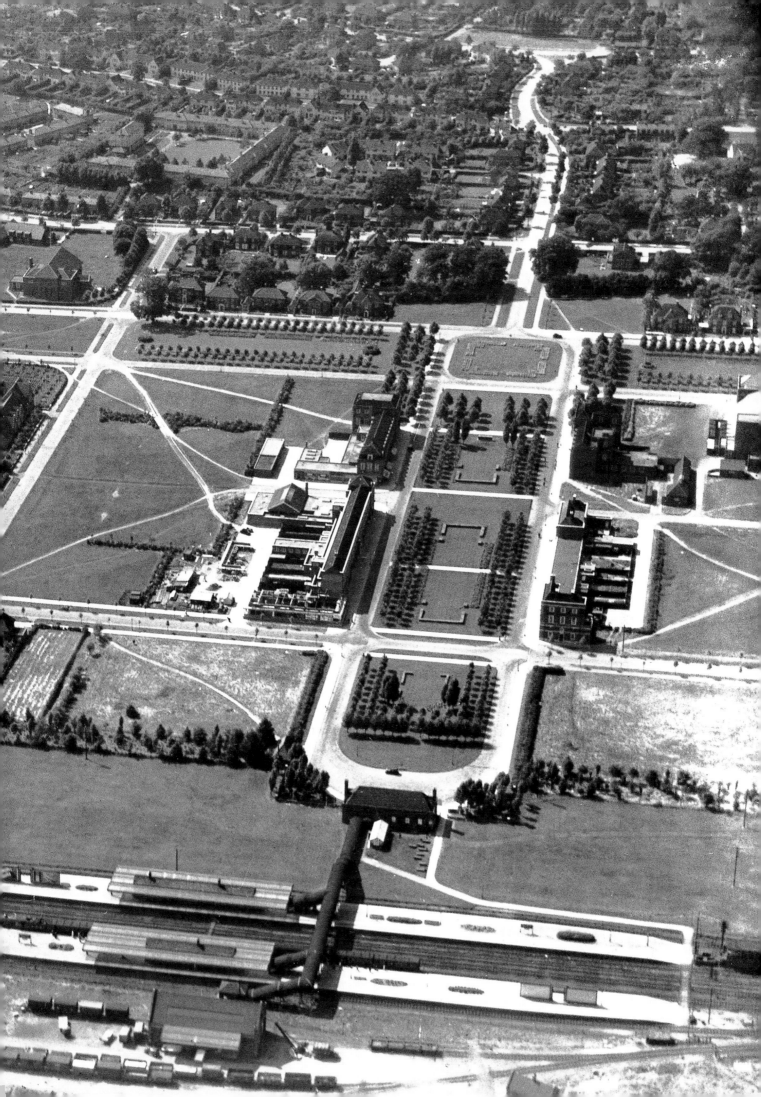

Wembley Park

With the famous twin towers of Wembley Stadium in the background at the end of Olympic Way, Wembley Park station on the line from Neasden to South Harrow can be seen in the foreground. The original line through Wembley Park — the Kingsbury & Harrow — was jointly promoted and owned by the Metropolitan and Metropolitan & St John's Wood railways and authorised on 16 July 1874. The 5.5-mile long route from Willesden Green to Harrow-on-the-Hill opened on 2 August 1880. The station at Wembley Park was opened in 1894. The line from Harrow-on-the-Hill from Neasden grew in importance with the opening of the Great Central's London Extension, to freight on 26 July 1898 and passenger services on 15 March 1899. Electric services over the Metropolitan were extended from Willesden Green to Wembley Park on 1 November 1906 and, until a further extension to Harrow on 19 July 1908, this was the point where the Metropolitan electric locomotives were replaced by steam. The Metropolitan line to Wembley Park was quadrupled in sections between 30 November 1913 and 31 May 1915 and extended northwards to Harrow-on-the-Hill on 10 January 1932. Slightly to the west of Wembley Park station is the junction for the Stanmore line; this was opened by the Metropolitan Railway in 1932 and transferred to the Bakerloo Line in 1932. It was to become part of the Jubilee Line in 1979. Today, passenger services at Wembley Park are provided by the Metropolitan and Jubilee lines, with Chiltern Trains' services passing non-stop.

26 April 1948 (R7824)

Wembley Stadium

It is 7 May 1955 and, in the background, the crowds
have thronged to Wembley Stadium to watch the 1955
FA Cup Final. In the foreground, of this view looking
towards the west, can be seen Wembley Stadium station,
which is located on the line from Neasden to Northolt
Junction. Called originally Wembley Hill when it opened
with the line, built by the Great Central Railway, on
1 March 1906; freight traffic along the line had
commenced on the previous 20 November. The station
became 'Wembley Complex' in the early 1970s and
gained its current name in 1988. The station, currently
served by Chiltern Line trains, remains open. The FA
Cup final was, incidentally, won by Newcastle United
who beat Manchester City 3-1.

7 May 1955 (A58472)

West Drayton

Viewed looking towards the east along the Great Western main line into Paddington, West Drayton station can be seen towards the top of the picture. Coming in from the north — the line swings round to the south and passes under the main line further west — is the branch to Staines West and in the foreground is the coal concentration depot. West Drayton was one of the original stations on Brunel's main line, opening with the route on 4 June 1838 (although the original station was located slightly to the west of the station illustrated here; it was relocated when the branch to Staines was opened). The Staines West branch was opened to Colnbrook on 9 August 1884 and to Staines on 2 November 1885; by the date of the photograph passenger services had been withdrawn — these had succumbed — on 29 March 1965 — but freight continued to run. The line continues to serve Colnbrook although the section between Colnbrook and Staines West was closed in the early 1980s as a result of construction of the M25. The curve of the branch visible here was originally constructed as the route of the GWR branch to Uxbridge; this had been authorised on 16 July 1846 and opened on 8 December 1856. Initially broad gauge, the branch was converted to standard gauge in 1871. However, by the date of the photograph, the line had closed: to passenger services on 10 September 1962 and to freight two years later except for a short section to serve the Middlesex Oil & Chemical Works that was reopened on 2 July 1966; this stub of the Uxbridge branch was to close on 8 January 1979.

16 March 1968 (A178361)

White City

The complex network of lines to the west of London on the West London line is clearly shown in this view taken towards the north. In the distance, the West London line itself can be seen heading towards Willesden Junction (1) as it passes over the ex-GWR main line towards Reading (2) and Paddington (4). From Old Oak East Junction (5) a spur can be seen heading to North Pole Junction (6) as well as a curve from North Pole Junction heading in the up direction towards Paddington. South of North Pole Junction, there were two stations called St Quintin Park & Wormwood Scrubs; the first opened in 1871 but this was relocated slightly to the north in 1893 and was to close on 1 December 1940. By the date of this photograph little remained of either station. To the south the Central Line from Ealing (9) can be seen approaching from the west; at Wood Lane Junction (8) a spur linked this line with the West London line at Viaduct Junction (7) with the Central line itself heading south towards White City (10). Further to the south, The Metropolitan Line from Paddington (15) can be seen passing through Latimer Road station (14), which opened four years after the line in 1868, before heading towards Hammersmith. The West London line itself continues south towards Kensington (12). Also visible is the site (13) of the Metropolitan Railway's spur between Latimer Road and the West London line, which permitted the Metropolitan to operate services to Addison Road; these were withdrawn on 20 October 1940 and the line closed completely from the same date. The history of the development of the lines in this area is covered in the section on Shepherd's Bush (see p194).

1 June 1963 (A112548)

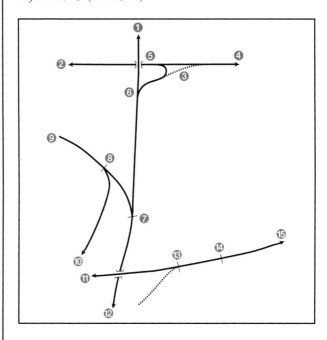

Whitechapel

Viewed looking towards the east, with Whitechapel Road stretching on into the Mile End Road, Whitechapel Underground station, used by the District and Metropolitan lines, can be seen in the left foreground. In the distance, running parallel to the Mile End Road can be seen the ex-GER main line from Liverpool Street heading towards Colchester. Authorised by the 1879 City Lines Act, the Metropolitan and District railways were permitted to construct a line from a triangular junction at Aldgate to Whitechapel; this line was opened on 6 October 1884 and enabled District and Metropolitan railway services to access the East London line via a curve located just to the west of the station illustrated here. The extension from the 1884 line, through the station illustrated, eastwards was authorised as the Whitechapel & Bow Railway in 1897; this line was designed to provide additional capacity from east London into the city as Fenchurch Street could not be enlarged. The line opened from Whitechapel to Campbell Road Junction on the LTSR on 2 June 1902 at which date the current Whitechapel station was also opened. The LTSR doubled its line between Campbell Road Junction and Barking. Heading north-south at this point, but sub-surface and therefore not visible in this view (the line emerges to the surface immediately to the north of the station but the route is shielded by buildings), is the East London line; this opened southwards from Wapping to New Cross Gate on 7 December 1869 and the northern extension, from Wapping, via Whitechapel, to Shoreditch opened on 10 April 1876.

19 June 1965 (A147200)

Willesden Junction

Situated on the West Coast main line between London Euston and Watford Junction, Willesden is one of the most important junctions located on the southern part of the route. Located in the foreground in this view taken looking towards the west, are the platforms of Willesden Junction (High Level) (1), (Low Level) (2) and (Main Line) (closed on 3 December 1962 and the platforms cleared soon afterwards in connection with the electrification project); (3) stations. The West Coast main line heads towards London (10) and Watford Junction (14), whilst at West London Junction (4) the ex-LNWR line towards Kensington (9). From the High Level platforms, one line heads towards Richmond (7) whilst at Willesden High Level Junction (15) a connection heads off to join the West London Line at Mitre Bridge Junction (8). Three sets of lines converge at Kensal Green Junction (6); these are the Up and Down City lines to the north heading towards Willesden Yard (11); the Up and Down Platform lines heading into High Level station en route to Richmond and the Up and Down New lines heading into Low Level and thence to Stonebridge Park (12). Beyond Kensal Green Junction the line heads on towards Gospel Oak (18). Just to the east of the station, the New lines are joined by the lines from Queens Park, which are also used by the Bakerloo Line trains of London Underground. Just to the east of the Main Line platforms, at North & South Western Junction (5), lines diverge from the West Coast main line to serve Willesden Yards (13) and Richmond (via Acton Wells Junction) (16). Also visible, under construction, is the depot (17) built to service the locomotives destined for use on the 25kV electrification of the West Coast route. The first railway to serve the area was the London & Birmingham, which opened north from Euston on 20 July 1837, although it was not until 1 September 1866 that a station called Willesden Junction opened. By that date much of the local infrastructure had already been completed; the line from North & South West Junction to Kew — later rerouted to Richmond — opened to freight on 15 February 1853 and to passenger services on 1 August 1853 whilst the Hampstead Junction (owned eventually by the LNWR but operated by the North London) opened through Willesden to Camden Town on 2 February 1860. The station was rebuilt in 1894 and further extended on 15 June 1912 with the opening of platforms to serve the New Lines, which also opened on that date north of Willesden to Harrow on the same day. Bakerloo Line services reached Willesden on 10 May 1915 and were extended north to Watford Junction on 16 April 1917.

9 March 1964 (A123992)

Wimbledon

Wimbledon was and is an important railway junction. Possessing 10 platform faces, at the time that this photograph was taken the local railway network had only just been completed — it was not until 7 July 1929 that the Wimbledon-South Merton section of the line to Sutton was opened (it was completed through to Sutton on the following 5 January) by the Southern Railway. The station illustrated shows the station as it existed after the modernisation of 1929 a decade later in connection with the Portsmouth line electrification. The view shows clearly the terminal platforms used by the District Railway — by this date under the control of the London Passenger Transport Board — with the ex-LSWR main line heading towards London. The District gained access to Wimbledon by exercising running powers over the LSWR from Putney. The first station at Wimbledon — known as Wimbledon & Merton until 1909 — was opened with the London & Southampton Railway's route from Nine Elms to Woking Common on 21 May 1838. The Wimbledon & Croydon Railway, incorporated in 1853, was opened on 22 October 1855 and was worked from the following year by the LBSCR. Authorised in 1864, the Tooting, Merton & Wimbledon Railway built a line from Streatham Junction to Wimbledon; at Tooting the line divided, with alternative routes reaching Wimbledon via Haydons Lane or via Merton Park on the line to Croydon. The TM&WR was jointly controlled by the LSWR and the LBSCR with the result that the section from Merton Park into Wimbledon passed to joint control. The line opened on 1 October 1868. District Railway trains first served Wimbledon on 3 June 1889 when the LSWR line between Wimbledon and Putney opened. The goods yard, which closed in January 1970, has disappeared, being replaced by the Centre Court shopping centre. District Line services continue to operate into the town whilst First Capital Connect services through the station on the ex-LSWR main line are in the hands of South West Trains. Services operated by Thameslink and Southern run into Wimbledon station over the ex-TM&WR line to the east and over the Sutton line to the west. However, the line from Wimbledon to Croydon has now been converted for use by Croydon Tramlink. Evidence of London's first generation of tramways can be seen as can one of the early trolleybuses, nicknamed 'Diddlers', that were introduced by London United Tramways in 1931.

5 May 1938 (57029)

Wimbledon Chase

Although promoted before the outbreak of World War 1, the line from Wimbledon to Sutton was not actually constructed until the 1920s. Powers were obtained in 1924, following agreement with the Underground not to extend the Northern line south of Morden, and the section of line from Wimbledon to South Merton opened on 7 July 1929 and from there to Sutton on 5 January 1930. The line was electrified from the start. This view of Wimbledon Chase station looking towards the junction with the LSWR main line at Wimbledon West Junction shows to good effect the standard design of the intermediate stations on the branch. Today the line is used primarily by First Capital Connect services although Southern also operates a limited number of services over the line.

2 July 1964 (A133054)

Aerofilms — A Brief History

Aerofilms was founded in 1919 as Britain's first commercial aerial photography company and over the years its Library has grown to over 750,000 oblique aerial images, taken in black and white until the early 1980s, and colour from the early '70s to date. Amongst the unique photographs are aerial views of Crystal Palace before its destruction in 1937, and the airship R-101 on its maiden flight in 1929.

The Aerofilms Library also holds the negatives of Aero Pictorial Ltd (1934-60) and Airviews of Manchester (1947-92), which together number close to 200,000. In addition, there are smaller collections of ground photography, chiefly from postcard companies such as Stearns, Lilywhite, and Overland.

Aerofilms was a pioneer in the field of vertical or 'survey' photography and its capabilities in this field meant the company was co-opted into the war effort in 1940, forming part of the Photographic Development Unit. After the war the company concentrated on oblique aerial photography until 1987, when it took over the business of its sister company Hunting Surveys Ltd, which had specialised in vertical photography. As a result, Aerofilms' library of vertical photographs spans from the late 1940s to date, including county surveys and more specialised low-altitude surveys of coastlines and rivers.

Today forming part of the Blom group, a pan-European mapping company, Simmons Aerofilms has offices in Cheddar and Potters Bar, whilst its three aircraft fly from Cranfield Airport near Milton Keynes.

Simmons Aerofilms Ltd
32-34 Station Close
Potters Bar
Herts EN6 1TL
Phone: 01707 648390
Fax: 01707 648399
E-Mail: library@aerofilms.com
www.simmonsaerofilms.com